D1626983

THEY OWN IT ALL
(Including YOU!)

By Means of Toxic Currency

written by:
Ronald MacDonald,
Robert Rowen, M.D.

"The surest way to overthrow an established social order is to debauch its currency."

Vladimir Lenin 1910, Founder of the Russian
Communist Party and architect of the Bolshevik Revolution.

"Lenin was certainly right, there is no more positive, or subtler, no surer means of overturning the existing basis of society than to debauch the currency ... The process engages all of the hidden forces of economic law on the side of destruction, and does it in a manner that not one man in a million is able to diagnose."

John Maynard Keynes, 1920, Economist, advisor to bankers, architect
of FDR's and America's "(deficit) spending one's way out of
bankruptcy".

This book provides the diagnosis (and the remedy).

www.NewPeopleOrder.com

NewPeopleOrder@gmail.com

IWantToHelpNewPeopleOrder@gmail.com

The economy is in a tumultuous meltdown. Our rights and liberties are being stripped right in front of our eyes. The establishment orders Congress "Put the taxpayers on the line "or else!""Virtually everything you now do is trackable, traceable, and can be used against you. In fact, there has just been legislation passed to enable taxing authorities access to some credit card transactions. The United States is off fighting foreign wars to spread the type of democracy we believe we have here. Has the "Brave New World" arrived without us knowing it?

This book will absolutely prove to you that the government and/or its agent have "invisibly" marked you. This mark isn't just a simple mark attached to each of us; it is an extraordinary mark that will blow your mind and **SHIFT YOUR REALITY!** You will find what the mark has done to you as **INCREDIBLE!** This mark moves with you and interfaces with **every** transaction you make. But like your childhood "invisible ink" becoming visible with heat, your invisible mark becomes visible simply with knowledge of what it is.

They **Own It All (Including You!)** explains to you in most simple common language the mark, the origin of the mark, and how it has relegated you/us to an unbelievable Brave New World status. *It identifies the mechanism of the mark as the singular cause of the financial crisis threatening your personal future and the future of the world's economies.* And, like all problems, when you can identify the cause, you have the ability to cure it.

We trust that you will enjoy it, be absolutely **SHOCKED** at what is revealed, and that you will quickly share the book with everyone you know. With knowledge spread among our population, the problem can be rectified before we are swallowed alive. You have nothing to lose. We have a duty to reveal it; you have a duty to learn it. And, by learning, you and our beleaguered population have everything to gain with knowledge of the hidden truth regarding all financial transactions. Website subscribers will automatically receive by email a short follow-up text on remedies to the problem. You can also download the free electronic business card to attach to all of your outgoing emails.

Your Authors: *Dr. Robert Rowen* **and** *Ronald MacDonald*

DISCLAIMER: None of the following information should be considered by the Reader as legal or medical advice. If one needs legal or medical advice, he must seek a professional in either area in accordance with the laws he finds himself a subject.

Dear Reader,

Few could deny the unfolding calamity working its way through the American and world economies. Is there any possibility that its real cause could be related to a most well known Biblical prophesy? Could that prophesy have nothing to do with the supernatural, but instead show the deepest insight into human **commercial** activity? Could seers 2,000 years ago have had better understanding of legal exchange among humans than our spoon-fed population? Could the fundamental cause of the collapse as well as your fate be kept hidden from you by deceit? **Are you not entitled to know the truth?** We certainly think so. When you understand the source of the unfolding financial calamity, so much more will be clear. The revelations you are about to discover are more priceless than flawless diamonds.

We have taken the liberty to liberally use the vernacular word the "Beast", or better put, "Bea$t" in this text. This common term, in our everyday language, and throughout history has been used to connote evil. It is important that no one be turned off by the colloquial term, as that is not the pivotal point of the message, nor is it meant to connote the supernatural. The message is that you have been marked with invisible ink by a greed in humans that cannot be even imagined without knowledge of it.

Much of what you are about to read you may already know. Though you may know the concepts, we humbly ask you to read through the entire book chapter by chapter until the end, even if the information is familiar to you. This is important in order to firmly connect the dots. With those dots connected, you'll at last see the truth. You'll see the whole story of the most ghastly event in American, if not human history. We will shock you that it was all perfectly "legal" in the jurisdiction of the bea$t, but unconscionable and fraudulent. That will arm you with the means to escape invisible bonds placed by a jailer that you cannot see, nor understand. There is remedy. The first step in remedy is to identify the problem. This book will provide you the means to see the invisible.

This book is written to reveal the main source of misery and suffering in America and also the world. Most important, no matter what you call the source that causes the misery and suffering, the greed is manifested by and through man upon man.

We are honored and grateful for your interest, and openness; and we hope that you will join with us in saving mankind from the darkness you are about to discover.

Robert Rowen, MD and *Ronald MacDonald*
October 1, 2008

DEDICATION

This book is dedicated to the thousands and perhaps millions of "Patriots" who stood up to the Bea$t and suffered without explanation. It is dedicated to the millions who have lost liberty or property in proceedings they knew were unjust, but had not a clue as to how it could happen "legally". It is dedicated to those who have lost their lives or have been injured at the hands of a force that placed profit above Life. And, it is dedicated to their spouses, families, friends, and other loved ones who suffered at their sides.

This book is also dedicated to every citizen of every country. What happened in America has happened in every country around the globe. The remedy is the same as for those in the United States.

DECLARATION

Both authors, Ronald Mac Donald and Robert Rowen state and make the following declaration: "We have researched and evidenced the facts written within $\mathfrak{They}$ **Own It All (Including You!)** except those items that would, to a reasonable man, be self-evident, and/or already known information. We cannot state for certain that it is the absolute truth, because none but the Creator shall make a declaration as such. However, we declare that it is the truth as we see it. We have not embellished upon what we, ourselves, know for certain."

Have we done due diligence? Yes, to the same degree any reasonable men could do the same. We believe that we have done this in the light of God. Perhaps we shall be found guilty of something. But it shall not be that we have had a modicum of malevolent intent in shouting truth to the *People.* We have felt an absolute compulsion to save this and other nations from the present and future dismal and perilous destiny so presently obvious to the world. Perhaps we could be found faulting. But it should not be for us having faith and belief in that what we have provided lacks truth.

Acknowledgements of Robert Rowen, MD

First and foremost I am grateful for the many blessings I have been given.

I give thanks and honor to my wife Terri, who has stood together with me with bravery and mettle. I honor and thank my family and friends who did not abandon me in times of great darkness, even while challenging my very unconventional ideas. They had to bear with me in fear for my livelihood and liberty during trying times in my 20-year path to discover the truth to unlock invisible shackles. Shackles placed on my chosen mission to minister healing to the sick. Shackles placed on everyone's ability to provide for their families. I further acknowledge my mentor and teacher, Ronald. It was his incredible legal mind, and never ending patience with me, that led to this priceless treasure of information that can liberate us all.

And I give thanks to all my many healing teachers who have taught me to seek the cause of illness in order to heal. The cause of illness is not a genetic deficiency of petrochemical drugs as virtually taught in pharmaceutical backed medical schools. The causes are mostly deficiencies of nutrients, an excess of empty calories and man-made toxins, injuries, and stress. Conventional medicine looks for the physical, what can be seen in an X-ray or other scan or lab test. If they are normal, it often assumes there is no problem. Then you receive a tranquilizer or other Band-Aid (usually toxic) approach to suppress symptoms. My mentors taught me to search for the invisible, and find it whenever possible. Then, with the cause made visible, you can be healed. I watched other like-minded healers destroyed by despotic and unreasonable regulatory authorities, even when the healers hurt no one. It was their pain and suffering that led me to the quest to uncover the force that placed these shackles on us, and you. And that quest led to uncovering one singular and invisible source – toxic currency.

Author *Robert Rowen* MD (RR)

ACKNOWLEDGEMENTS OF RONALD MACDONALD

I give thanks for all of my blessings. I further give thanks to my wife Pam, daughters Franki and Chelsea, and future son-in-law, Justin, all of whom fulfill my life, and to the co-author, Robert, for appearing in my life for the purpose of a messenger and a revealer of the truth.

I acknowledge you also (the reader), because you have purpose in my life as I in yours. Further, I wish to pass two thoughts to the reader as he journeys through this book. "If a man is not willing to die for his principles, then he has no principles, and deserves to be within the status of a farm animal, with the farmer's authority over his every moment. Those men who hide in the shadows while others dart into the light are deserving of their slaughter when the axe of the farmer befalls their necks." That said, I would request that each take courage in the pursuit of truth, because remaining within the lie is the greatest of miseries, and not even the pain or moment of death is its equal.

The second thought, if you cannot see the Beast, do you expect to see his mark? You must expect the mark to be *invisible*, for if it is not *invisible*, you have the power to rip it from you!

Author *Ronald MacDonald* (RM)

At Personal Peril

We both realize that exposing truth, especially truth like this, can come at significant risk (see appendix I). We pondered using fictitious names in order to protect ourselves from possible reprisals. Our families urged us to do so as well. Yet how could we expect any honorable people to stand up to the Bea$t if we, ourselves, knowing the truth will not take up the front line at personal peril? Could we expect the reader to do so if we do not?

We know not what fate shall befall us, but this we know with certainty, "If a man is not willing to die for the truth, then he is willing to live a lie!" We are willing (but not desiring) to die for the truth!

Should your authors suffer peril at the hands of unseen power, then and at that time, you not only are granted license to reproduce this book and profit from the selling of it personally, but you have the duty to perform this task to make the invisible truth visible to all eyes! Should you not do this, then be reminded of the dilemma of many who fell victim to evil in World War II. By not standing to protect the innocent, there was no one left to protect those who stood by in silence.

Our spirits will be at far greater rest knowing we have stimulated the return to honest money. We will rest further knowing that the **New People Order** has established a new hierarchy of the People as the Master, and the government as the servant, as our Founders intended.

RR and RM

DOWNLOAD FREE SEQUEL AND REMEDY

Please sign up for the free sequel and remedy to **They Own It All (Including You!).** Simply visit www. NewPeopleOrder.com and leave your name and email address to get the free download of the sequel and remedy.

PURPOSE

"Disobedience to tyranny is obedience to God." (Benjamin Franklin, most famous of the Founding Fathers and whose image appears on a $100 bill)

The purpose of this book is to absolutely prove to you that you, right here and now, wear the "Mark of the Beast" as literally described almost two thousand years ago. This is **not** a religious issue. Think about current events. Almost everyone knows that there is something wrong with America, something dreadfully wrong. But we can't put our finger on it. Events are spinning out of control. There is near total loss of confidence in the government that was once trusted. People are in fear. Why has the trust faded? Is there a subconscious realization that there is something fundamentally awry with government?

We have chosen the theme ("beast") because the concept has been widely known and watched for hundreds of years. Is it possible that our ancestors really knew what was to befall us? Is it possible that they somehow understood the unseen dangers and we somehow have been unable to? No matter your religion, spiritual path, or personal philosophy, we will show you that all of us are carrying the mark. It appears it was predicted in the following writing:

"And he causeth all, both small and great, rich and poor, free and bond, to receive a mark in their right hand, or in their foreheads:

And that no man might buy or sell, *save he that had the mark, or the name of the beast, or the number of his name."* Rev. 13:17-18

Buying and selling is not a <u>*religious*</u> ritual. It is survival. It is economics. The warning was not directed to any religion or religious group. It predicted something grave to happen to all men. As we said, Americans do know that something is desperately wrong with current economics. We (authors) unequivocally state that all of us carry an invisible "legal" mark, to which if attention is directed, becomes instantly visible. Remember when you were a child writing with "invisible ink" (lemon juice)? It became visible with the light and heat of a candle. Please permit us to be a candle to light your way through the maze of a totally corrupt monetary system that has tagged you with an invisible ink that we will rename.

Please read this book in that light. If you can disprove our claim that you do not bear such a mark, we will cheerfully refund you the price of the book. We ask that you please read this book chapter by chapter. Each chapter provides a foundation for the next. Jumping forward will undermine the foundation of your understanding. With a firm knowledge of the truth of the cause of sickness, remedy can be had. And, for the invisible mark you carry, there are very powerful remedies, the most important of which is you.

PROLOGUE

"I have ways of making money that you know nothing of. ... I would rather earn 1% off a 100 people's efforts than 100% of my own efforts."
– John D. Rockefeller

You are in a bad way. Times are real hard. People are out of work. You can barely feed your family. A dragon (bea$t) comes to your door in full regalia. He's snorting and breathing fire. The pungent smell of smoldering cinders permeates the air. He tells you he's the keeper of souls. He has an offer for you. "I have a lot of these very special pieces of paper (bank issued currency). They are very popular. People all over the world covet them. They can get you most anything you want. Wine, food, women, song, cars, diamonds, even houses and a yacht." You ask, what's the bottom line? He says "your soul. That's the whole deal, no hidden extras" You are desperate for your family and take the deal.

Question: "Did a wrong occur here?" Yes, but not how you might think. Was the dragon (bea$t) evil? No. You knew exactly who he was. He had a contract to offer, fully disclosed with terms and conditions. He did not lie, cheat, steal, or beguile. Believe it or not, that's the type of "person" we, the authors, would want to contract with. It's because all of the facts are presented honestly. It is our personal choice to sign or not sign a deal made with full and open disclosure.

If there was evil in this deal, we believe it was you, for trading in your soul for material wealth.

Now consider this alternate example. You are in a bad way. Times are real hard. Many people are out of work and going hungry. So are you. The dragon (bea$t) disguises himself. He takes on an ordinary human form, man or woman, and puts on a suit. He comes to your door with an offer. "I have lots of these very special pieces of paper (bank issued currency). They are very popular and people all over the world covet them. They can get you most anything you want – wine, food, women, song, cars, diamonds, even houses and a yacht. All you have to do is *pay me back plus a little interest.*" Despite the soft-spoken words, you did hear them. You ask, "What happens if I can't make the payments?" He says, "Hey, there are plenty of these papers around. I'm sure that you'll get what you need from your business with others. Besides, you can always file bankruptcy."

Hey, what a deal! You take it. Now what the bea$t didn't tell you is that all the pieces of paper everyone else has also have an interest burden. The dragon created, let's say, 100 pieces of paper, and the interest is 5%. So, with only the principle out there how is he going to be paid back plus the interest? The interest of five extra pieces of paper currency doesn't exist! Someone will go down, just for you to get the interest to pay your share. Oh, he also didn't tell you that you couldn't bankrupt **_his_** pieces of paper, just everyone else's. See, he was the source of the papers. He can't be bankrupted. You can only bankrupt other users of the paper. But they were counting on your business to help them pay their interest. You bankrupted them. Now, they can't pay and lose everything. Or, they bankrupt you, you can't pay the bea$t, and he takes everything from you!

Oh, and he didn't tell you the most important part of all. On these pieces of paper is a dragon $lime that to humans is odorless, colorless, tasteless and otherwise totally imperceptible. It slides off and marks you. Even worse, the $lime on the documents self executes and perpetuates, even in the dragon's absence. When you pass off the piece of paper to everyone else, the $lime marks them as well, as it does with each subsequent pass off. You extend your right hand to receive and pass off his papers. The $lime of his invisibly marked papers marks (brands) your hand. It invisibly slips off and $limes (marks) everything you will ever acquire. When you transfer the papers to the next receiver, it contaminates him/her as well. And so on, forever with each new user. It creates the illusion that you are free and independent. Yet in truth, all the time you are working for the bea$t. You unknowingly become subject to strange rules and regulations limiting your freedom since you are marked by the $lime. You don't ever know those rules and regulations are really his. If you violate his rules and regulations, he will send his collectors immediately to take what is his. That includes anything and everything, including you, that has been marked by the $lime.

Is there evil in this deal? Absolutely. You were given a contract with terms and conditions unrevealed (fraudulently concealed). That is evil, pure and simple. You, unknowingly, took on his mark branding you. But far worse, you have become his agent spreading his mark universally to others without their knowledge or consent. There could never be a more diabolical plan, for it represents the enslavement or capture of all humanity, with your unwitting assistance.

The purpose of this book is to place before you the facts and evidence much of which you already know. However, until now there have been many dots unconnected. We will connect them for you. Then we will let you be the jury and try the facts we have given you. They will prove to you beyond reasonable doubt, that you have been anointed with the Mark of the Bea$t as per the **_second_** example above, and that you are owned by "them."

Many people in America think that there's no escape from the quickening pace of loss of freedom. There isn't freedom without knowledge: "My People perish from lack of knowledge" (Hosea 4 v 6). When the blinders are lifted you will see the $lime and the mark of the bea$t, that would otherwise cause us to perish. You will take steps to wash it off. You'll assist others to do the same. The Truth will set you Free.

Introduction

The Beast and the Mark

Most Christians recognize the term "beast" to mean the evil one or Satan. Satan is not a stranger to most religions. Indeed he is in the Hebrew Old Testament right in the Garden of Eden. There, _disguised_ as a serpent, he tricked Eve into eating of the forbidden fruit. Satan appears in the Koran and New Testament. In the Hindu religion, the universe is a balance of good and evil. All religions speak of a duality in the physical universe. Perhaps because of the Bible, the serpent came to be the personification of evil. Is it any wonder that popular former President Andrew Jackson referred to a great evil he saw as "a den of vipers" (quote at head of chapter 16) and promised to rout it out? We choose a less religious term for evil – "bea$t". We take the liberty of using the pronoun "it" to refer to "the bea$t." And, as you will discover, the "**bea$t**" is not supernatural.

We also recognize two metaphysical principles. One is that **truth** operates in the light with full disclosure. And the other is that a **lie** must operate concealed and hidden in the shadows for success to be had against its subject.

Let's examine this logically. Suppose an evil dragon were really to appear to you breathing fire. Would that constitute a trick or beguiling? Would you enter into a contract with him? If yes, most people would describe you as "blithing crazy!" Clearly you would not be tricked or beguiled were it to physically manifest to you. It appears the bea$t would have to operate in shadows (invisible) to exert its powers. It is ludicrous to think that evil would openly reveal itself.

Now we accept the premise that the prophesized mark is a mark of wickedness.

So, what is a mark anyway? Farley's Free dictionary online tells us a mark may be:

> *a. An inscription, name, stamp, label, or seal placed on an article to **signify ownership**, quality, manufacture, or origin.*

A wolf marks his territory by spraying (urinating) on the land he claims. A ranch, say the Subterfuge Ranch may mark its animal with a brand "S". The "mark" signifies ownership.

Many take the term "'mark' of the beast" to mean a physical mark. This might include an implanted chip, a social security number, or some other identifier that you would know as his mark.

But wait a moment. The bea$t is the beguiler or trickster. That which deceives, must remain in shadows. So why on earth would it put a physical mark on you? There would be no tricking. The plot would be plain and openly revealed. For example, would the bea$t physically brand you with his "S" like a rancher brands his cows? Clearly the brand of the rancher identifies the cow as his chattel (property). That cow is known to all as the property of say the Subterfuge Ranch.

Would the bea$t do that? Heck, if he did, his gig would be up. No beguiling! There's just no way.

Hence, like the invisible evil force, the mark must tag you, but not visibly. To match the **prediction** it must follow you and be part of all your economic transactions. Without it, you would not be able to buy or sell. Try looking in the mirror for the mark. We assure you that you won't see it. But we will prove you have been anointed with such a mark, by trickery!

TABLE OF CONTENTS

THIS BOOK WILL PROVE TO YOU THAT ALL CURRENCY IN THE WORLD IS TOXIC RESULTING IN THE FOLLOWING:

1. You are legally a debtor and chattel (property) owned by a hidden creditor.
2. There is a hidden lien on everything transacted for by or with a Federal Reserve Note.
3. Your entire alleged wealth is/has been liened, you don't own anything! You merely have possession by privilege. This privilege may be yanked at any time if you don't obey the real owner.
4. The Federal Reserve Note is a foreign product owned by a foreign corporation, and not by you or the U.S. government.
5. The States and the United States courts are bankruptcy courts representing the interests and property of the foreign creditor.
6. Without knowing it, you have been compelled into international commercial law, where you have none of your unalienable rights. Hence, you have been insulated from your birthright, the common Law from which your rights are immutable.
7. You are charged an income (excise) tax for transacting in the foreign commodity known as Federal Reserve Notes.
8. You have been divested of the rights to, value of, and profits from your labor, which has been stolen.
9. Lawful gold coin (pre 1933) money transactions are invisible to the states and national government(s).
10. The real cause of draconian governmental regulation and your loss of rights is the toxic currency.
11. The United States lost its sovereignty in 1933. It is in receivership to the hidden creditor. The bankrupt government is a puppet to the real master, as declared by Banker Rothschild on the cover.
12. The real cause of the current economic calamity is the toxic currency.
13. The hidden creditor (international bankers) owns everything, including you.
14. You have been living within an illusion, believing that you are free, but in reality you are owned!

With this knowledge comes the singular remedy!

CHAPTER 1

USURY

"In thee have they taken gifts to shed blood; thou hast taken usury and increase, and thou hast greedily gained of thy neighbours by extortion, and hast forgotten me, saith the Lord GOD."
– (Ezekiel 22:12)

We use the Bible as a reference point for moral relations with our fellow man, and how that flows into our modern law and unalienable rights. Few people on the planet have not heard of or read the Ten Commandments.

The first 4 were commandments regarding the honoring of God. The remaining 6 set a foundation by which to live our lives harmoniously among our fellow men. The rules were simple. So simple that any person would know the rules even if he never heard of the "Ten Commandments". Why? Our conscience. We certainly know the difference between right and wrong, good and evil. We inherently know that it is wrong to steal, to bear false witness, to murder, etc.

Some religious teachings tell us that there is but one sin against man – theft. If you murder, you have stolen a man's life. If you lay with his wife, you have stolen his marriage. If you bear false witness, you have stolen the victim's future or his property or his freedom. And if you borrow something from someone and do not return it, have you not committed theft? Coveting is mental theft (greed is mental theft). Even if you lost the lender's possession, simply not returning it is tantamount to stealing. That is the basis of holding one who is a debtor and cannot pay his debt as having committed a crime, the crime of theft. He is called "insolvent". The term means one who cannot pay his debt as agreed. Once upon a time there used to be debtor's prisons. Debtors committed theft: grounds for imprisonment. You may think that these prisons have vanished. You have been beguiled. The prison has taken another form, not physical, as you will soon see.

The Bible also provided us the most basic rule of economics: the prohibition of usury. For centuries, usury has been known as the practice of lending money for interest. Many theologies prohibit usury. The Bible repeatedly forbids it. Why? And why has the definition been altered in recent times to prohibit "excessive" interest rather than prohibit interest altogether?

Consider that you are in the lending business. You lend a man a hoe to work his field. How is he able to return 2 hoes? They do not reproduce! To charge interest in the form of a hoe commands him to an impossible task. He will not be able to repay the debt. That's easy to see.

But suppose you lend him $100,000 and charge a 10% yearly interest. Any person in today's society knows that over 30 years that will translate into $300,000 or perhaps much more. Considering that only $100,000 was actually printed somewhere, where does the rest of the money come from that was not actually printed? More interest will be ultimately generated than there will be money printed to pay it back! When the money can't be paid back, the borrower goes into default. He loses everything. Worse, if what he has cannot cover the outstanding principle, he is insolvent. In Biblical law, he becomes the property of the lender until he can pay off the loan. Why? Insolvency is the <u>crime</u> of theft.

Now suppose I loan you $100 with the following terms of the loan:

1. Each dollar note is marked.
2. Each person who subsequently touches any of these notes must pay a charge for the use of that note(s), and these transactions go on FOREVER with each note.
3. Everything that you buy with the use of that note is liened until the note is paid back.

Let's say I lend a $100 note and that the $100 note carries a use fee of 10%. And, let's say the single $100 note, gets passed around 100 times in the next year. And each time it passes from one to another, 10% is charged to each who has used the $100 note. I would then surely end up with a great return from the money I lent. I get $10 one hundred times or $1000 return on my loan of $100. And even better, the $100 is still out there generating more use fees. The debt, which is the 10% I earn (that is payable to me) every time the $100 passes between people, is reproducing or multiplying exponentially. Now you can see why usury was historically forbidden. While one person might be able to repay, society as a whole cannot. It is impossible because only the $100 note exists and no extra notes were printed to pay the exponential interest that continues to build. Even a low rate of interest creates a debt that cannot be repaid. Usury is the perfect means to capture a population. The one who creates a debt that cannot be repaid becomes the ruler of all who are in debt.

Chapter 2

Consequences of Debt

"I, however, place economy among the first and most important republican virtues, and public debt as the greatest of the dangers to be feared."
(Thomas Jefferson, 3rd U.S. President)

There is no sin in borrowing. You might need to borrow your neighbor's plow if yours breaks and its planting season. However, you must return it. You owe him one plow. Not to return it is theft.

Our legal heritage is the common law, which is built from peoples' customs from antiquity. It is the unwritten law that everyone knows without being told. Common law has its roots from well before and within the Ten Commandments and the golden rule. Hence, a common law crime could be murder, theft, assault, rape, etc.

Imagine the year is 1820. You borrow money allegedly to build a house. You gamble away the money instead. Now you are insolvent and can't pay a thing or offer any collateral. You are now an insolvent debtor. Did this not constitute theft?

To be an insolvent debtor is a common law crime. It does constitute theft. The creditor could, if he wished, imprison the debtor, you, until the debt was paid.

Have you ever heard of the word "chattel"? In an early American law dictionary (Bouvier, 1853), it was defined as "property". Your cow would be considered your chattel. But have you ever considered that a man could be chattel, that is, property of someone else? Now we are not talking slavery here. That's totally different. We are talking about lawful (within the common law) chattel. Slavery, in our opinion, is a violation of rights of all men. It forcibly violates another man's Liberty. But suppose you voluntarily enter into a contract with someone. A loan is a contract. If you violate the terms of that contract, you can and should be held to perform. One man gave you something and you did not return it in kind. Again, this is theft.

The common law provided a penalty for debt. You must "PAY UP!" Let's see exactly how this was done. We again turn to Bouvier's Law Dictionary for more regarding chattel:

> *"Debtors taken in execution, captives, apprentices, are accounted chattels."*

Read this again: "Debtors taken in 'execution' (of their debt)…are chattels (property).

What does Bouvier tell us about "execution"? In this context that we are using it, it's not an assassination:

Execution means *"contracts". The accomplishment of a thing; as the execution of a bond and warrant of attorney, which is the signing, sealing, and delivery of the same.*

So, the debtor is taken by the creditor for not accomplishing and delivering the contract (debt re-payment) he entered into, and as such, he becomes the chattel or property of the creditor. As chattel, debtors have no rights. They have the privileges granted by the creditor. The creditor can keep him out of jail provided that the debtor obeys the creditor's regulations for limited liberty. The creditor would give his chattel license (permission) to do things for which the debtor would need no such permission had he not been a debtor. The creditor's concern was in collecting what was his. After the debt was paid, the man, no longer a debtor, was free.

The creditor might give the debtor notes to use to acquire the necessities of life. That way he could continue to work off the debt. All money he would acquire would be the property of the creditor until the debt was paid.

Are you familiar with the Biblical phrase that the sins of the father shall be visited upon the children? Just as parents could pass down their holdings, they also passed on their debts. The Bible is full of laws that have flowed to our current legal system. One was to avoid corruption against the blood (family and Nation).

Let's see how Bouvier defines corruption:

CORRUPTION. *An act done with an intent to give some advantage inconsistent with official duty and the rights of others. It includes bribery, but is more comprehensive; because an act may be corruptly done, though the advantage to be derived from it be not offered by another.* Merl. Rep. h.t.

2. By corruption, sometimes, is understood something against law; as, a contract by which the borrower agreed to pay the lender usurious interest. It is said, in such case, that it was corruptly agreed, &c.

Are the family and Nation corrupted by debt that renders them subservient to a creditor and with passage on to children and community? Is not the Lender who deliberately inflicts this corruption (bondage by debt), the epitome of greed?

Chapter 3

Common Law and Commercial Law

"The Common Law of England has been laboriously built about a mythical figure—the figure of 'The Reasonable Man'."
(Sir Alan Patrick Herbert, English novelist, law reform activist, and Oxford's Member of Parliament)

The common law of England is also known as the law of the land. It is the birthright of all Americans. It was enshrined in the Magna Charta, which is also known as the Great Charter and cornerstone of English liberty.

This nation was founded from British colonies. People were on the land. They were not in commerce, but traded amongst themselves. For these matters, God was their Sovereign and Benefactor. You might be interested to know that when the ancient Israelites established a king, they granted him limited powers. His power was to protect his people. He did not retain personal sovereignty over individuals. Their Sovereign was God. God's laws, which later became the "common law," were their laws.

Common law requires both an action and an injury in order to punish the alleged perpetrator by personal retribution or in court. An action, such as name calling, jay walking, or remodeling your house without a permit doesn't damage another man. Stealing his hoe does cause injury. You have denied him use of his hoe. Assaulting him injures him.

The difference is clear. The concept that the common law requires not only an action but an actual injury to another man is important. One will find these kinds of crimes, those without an injury/damage, in the Commercial Law, which is also known as Administrative Law. Here is an example where no one is injured in the violation of the commercial law: The failure to stop at a traffic light or stop sign when you can clearly see no one is in view doesn't harm anyone. (However, we don't suggest doing it!). A California billboard states, "Click it" (seatbelt) "or tic-ket" (penalty). There is/are no damage(s)/injury(ies) with these. So the ticket you receive from the camera or hidden cop isn't a common law matter. It is commercial/administrative law – and all administrative law is PENAL (Penalty) in nature. As will be made clear, we live in what could be called a Penal Colony where every activity of a man is subject to regulation. And, every violation of a regulation has a corresponding penalty attached. Of course the creditor is just demanding that you protect his chattel (you). We will revisit this.

Commercial law is also known as the law of the sea. This is the law which was ordained by man. Commercial law is not the People's customs, which customs are also known as common law. Commercial law involves the transport of goods, commodities, and property across fictional borders, which are the borders between countries, for resale on the homeland. There are 2 jurisdictions (types of law) in commercial law – Admiralty and Maritime. They are essentially the same. They are defined as the law of contract (commercial law) on the high seas. Maritime is commercial law in a time of peace. Admiralty is commercial law in a time of war or emergency.

To be in commerce was a privilege that could be taxed. Why? There were pirates on the sea from which you would need protection. You needed ports built for delivery of your goods. The people on the land could be impacted by what you brought in. For example, you might bring in oranges from Brazil grown with cheap labor that would put the people in Florida out of work, if they were growing oranges at a higher cost. You might bring in diseased goods. The people granted government the power to regulate commerce. Part of that was the power to impose taxes and duties on commercial activities to raise revenue. Merchants paid for these protections by paying customs, duties and imposts. These are also called excise taxes for the privilege of engaging in commerce.

In commercial law, you could be punished for action only, even without injury. For example, if the government deemed that something should not be imported for whatever reason, and you did in fact import it, you could be punished. If your truck, which was operated on the highways, was overweight, even if there was no mishap, you could be punished. There is merit to this. Would you want some truck unsafely hauling, for profit, 3 trailers to put your family at risk on the roads? No, such activities need to be regulated. We will cover this more in the chapter on administrative law.

Again, Admiralty/maritime jurisdictions are strictly international contract law on the sea. Here is what Bouvier's Law Dictionary (1853) said about Admiralty/Maritime:

ADMIRALTY. *The name of a jurisdiction which takes cognizance of suits or actions which arise in consequence of acts done upon or relating to the sea; or, in other words, of all transactions and proceedings relative to commerce and navigation, and to damages or injuries upon the sea. In the great maritime nations of Europe, the term "admiralty jurisdiction," is, uniformly applied to courts exercising jurisdiction over maritime contracts and concerns.*

MARITIME. *That which belongs to or is connected with the sea.*

MARITIME CAUSE. *Maritime causes are those arising from maritime* **contracts**, *whether made at sea or on land, that is, such as relate to the commerce, business or navigation of the sea; as, charter parties, affreightments, marine loans,* **hypothecations**… *and jettisons; contracts relating to marine insurance, and those between owners of ships. 3 Bouv. Inst. n. 2621. (Emphasis added)*

We will revisit Admiralty/Maritime again when we review the powers granted to the national government. Please remember that Admiralty pertains to contracts related to the sea or international contracts. Also note the word *hypothecations*. We know that it's most likely you never heard that word before. Just remember for now that maritime law can arise from hypothecations.

CHAPTER 4

COMMON LAW, PROPERTY, AND THE PAYMENT OF DEBT

"Interest works night and day in fair weather and in foul. It gnaws at a man's substance with invisible teeth."
(Henry Ward Beecher, mid 19th century clergyman
and social reformer) [Invisible teeth belong to
the Beguiler! - authors]

The common law was very clear in human transactions. We are to be fair, honest and equitable in our transactions with our fellow man. We were commanded to pay substance for substance. Of course, your payment might be an hour of labor for a meal. It might be a painting for a piece of furniture. But not everyone had the identical thing to exchange that was needed by the trading partner. Hence, a medium of exchange was ordained. It had to be in limited supply and could not be easily manufactured. In the common law gold and silver coin fit the bill. These are metals that come from the earth itself, and are valued by humans for their beauty and scarcity. They represent both form **and** substance. Form as the shape of a thing. Substance means mass or density - physical presence. Gold and silver come from the earth. They are literally **portable** (easily moved about) land. Hence, when you pay for something in gold, you are exchanging land (substance) for what you purchase. Gold, more rare and beautiful, became the money of Kings and Sovereigns. Silver, being less scarce, became the money of the masses.

Concerning the value of gold and silver, it is the relative scarcity which maintains the STEADY value of these precious metals. The only reason for a **product** to rise in "value" is the scarcity of it. When a new subdivision of homes opens on an island the first offering of homes may be for $100K. As the land and homes on the island begin to sell, the prices on the land/homes rise. The scarcity governs the price. Once the island is completely sold, the resale value, assuming the island is a very desirable location, will rise based on the law of supply and demand. Thus, the scarcity of gold and silver maintains their values.

In the common law you would negotiate a contract say for a cow. When you gave the seller a piece of gold (or silver) for his cow, the debt was paid and immediately extinguished. There was no recourse. It was a contract that was satisfied by both parties, instantaneously. Now while we say there was no recourse, that's not absolute.

Consider this scenario. As you walked away with your cow, you discover that it was branded by the Subterfuge Ranch. The cow was not the seller's at all to sell. The following day, the cow is repossessed by the ranch agents. They inform you that the cow was stolen. A fraud was committed upon you by the alleged "seller". Yes, you would have redress in courts of common law. Furthermore, the common law itself provides you a remedy. The man committed theft. You would be entitled to track him down yourself and personally extract from the thief what he stole from you, without police, judges, and attorneys!

Paying in gold immediately and forever extinguishes the debt and ends the transaction. There is no right of return, even if you changed your mind. However, if the seller concealed something of material importance to you, such as the car was liened, or the odometer set back, or had been in a serious accident, you would have remedy. This would be a fraud, which constitutes theft. You could take the fraudulent seller to task.

In the common law, your property was yours. You had absolute title, rights, and interest in the property. You paid for the property with your gold, over which you were sovereign and absolute owner. You had absolute title, rights, and interest in your gold. Those 3 inherent qualities instantly transfer into the thing you bought, extinguishing the debt. You were king of your holdings/properties. You have a right and duty to protect it - even with lethal force. If an intruder broke into your house, you could shoot him on the spot. After all, a crime was being perpetrated against you.

Consider that today; you don't have the right to shoot an intruder. You might go to jail for protecting what you "think" is yours. If you have loose wiring and a thief electrocutes himself, he can sue you. A parent could be negligent in the care of his child. The child might wander onto your property and fall into your pool. You can be sued for not having a fence up, even though the child had trespassed onto your property. The state has become a party to events that transpire on what you think is your property. How? There are startling legal reasons for this you will soon discover.

Substance   *Common Law*

CHAPTER 5

"There in no virtue so truly great and godlike as justice."
(Joseph Addison) *"Justice consists not in being neutral between right and wrong, but in finding out the right and upholding it, wherever found, against the wrong."*
(Theodore Roosevelt, 26th U.S. President)

One of the great symbols in our nation and the courts is the so-called "scale of justice". Some allege that the scale actually symbolizes the scale of Solomon in the Bible. What did that scale represent? You might think that it was a balance of facts to render a decision. Indeed it was not. On one side of the scale was the law (Law of Moses or common law). And, on the other side was gold! You cannot have law without gold. Gold could not be corrupted. Men paid their debts with gold. Law was/is about contract. Contract always involves property and/or payment. Payment was gold! Hence, the balance scale: law (contract) on one side, and the fulfillment of the contract with payment on the opposite side!

Chapter 6

"Nothing is so well calculated to produce a death-like torpor in the country as an extended system of taxation and a great national debt."
(William Cobbett, 19th century English political pamphleter, farmer and journalist)

On the land, within the common law, people paid their debts on the spot. That was never the case with merchants and for good reason. Suppose that you owned a ship laden with furniture. You arrive in port. You unload the boat of its cargo and now need to be paid. If the receiver was waiting for you with gold, he would be a target for robbery. If thieves knew that you were returning with a chest full of gold, you would be a target. It was awkward and inconvenient to carry heavy loads of precious metal for payment in commercial transactions.

Another means of transaction was required. It's called a Bill of Exchange (BoE). In the alternative, you could issue a promissory note (PN), a promise to pay.

A BoE is quite simple. It's a demand by one party to a third party to pay a second party a certain sum by a specific date. You know this in your own life simply as a bank check. You (first party) have ordered the bank (third party) to pay a specific amount to whom (second party) you wrote the check to by a specific date (checks are good for 6-12 months).

A BoE does not, and never did constitute payment. It was merely a **discharge** of an obligation. The BoE gave the receiver the means to get paid. A BoE is essentially a check. It's like you giving a check for payment of a coat. The check has to be negotiated and the bank make payment. After the seller got the BoE, the buyer was relieved of his responsibility in commercial law. The remedy for the seller was to negotiate the BoE for actual payment (substance). Then, and only then, the debt would be extinguished. Until that happened, the debt was merely "discharged" from the person issuing the bill of exchange. The debt still existed until the paper was redeemed. In your case, if your check is returned marked "insufficient funds" the seller would not be pleased and would come for actual payment.

It is the same thing with a PN. It represented money, money owed. BoE and PN could be exchanged among merchants. You could issue a BoE or PN for a "purchase". The merchant could exchange the note for another purchase, and so on. The note might not get redeemed for months or longer, but they were redeemable.

These paper instruments became known as "monetary instruments". They were not money. They "represented" money. They became the essence of commercial transactions.

Representations of money were passed around. Commerce was not substance for substance. Unlike the law of the land, exchanges were made with representations of money. There was benefit for the buyer and seller alike. A stolen note could be replaced. A stolen note could be reported to the person who issued it. Payment would be stopped. Today, you can report to the bank that your check was stolen. That prevents the thief from cashing (redeeming) it.

An excellent movie is, "Rob Roy". In fact, that movie, which takes place in 1700s England, gives you an outstanding example of notes, gold, debt, payment, and consequences of debt in an entertaining Hollywood presentation. Stolen gold could not be replaced.

CHAPTER 7

COMMERCIAL LAW AND NON-PAYMENT OF DEBT

"It is a terrible situation when the Government, to insure the National Wealth, must go in debt and submit to ruinous interest charges, at the hands of men, who control the fictitious value of gold. Interest is the invention of Satan."
(Thomas Edison, American inventor of electric light bulb)

Suppose you arrive at port with your loaded ship and the merchant buyer, who is waiting on the dock, cannot pay you for the goods. You have a problem. You can return to your country with the fully loaded ship and nothing to show for it. Or, you can unload the cargo and give it to the merchant. However, the goods are not paid for. Nevertheless, you do receive promissory notes from him for the goods. This constitutes a loan from you, the seller to the buyer. You must trust the buyer's promise to pay. But in commercial law, the buyer just doesn't get to walk away with the goods simply tendering/offering a promise to pay. You, the creditor, retain a claim against the goods. The goods are attached by what is called a "maritime hypothecation". A maritime hypothecation means a lien, until the goods are paid for in full. We mentioned 'hypothecation' in *Chapter 3*. This term is likely foreign to you. So, let's turn to Bouvier's Law Dictionary to fully understand it.

HYPOTHECATION, *civil law. This term is used principally in the civil law; it is defined to be a right which a creditor has over a **thing** belonging to another, and which consists in the power to cause it to be sold, in order to be paid his claim out of the proceeds.*

In maritime law, you may have sold a "thing" off your ship to the merchant standing on the dock. The merchant may walk away with those things in his "possession." However, if he has not paid you for those things, they still belong to you. Moreover, to prove that those things that are in his possession still belong to you, you have placed an attached lien upon them. This is hypothecation. You are not only the owner of the lien but also the owner of those things until they are paid for in full. And, if they are not eventually paid for, you have the right to seize those things. You can cause them to be sold in order to have your lien paid. Even if he gave you a note of credit, say from a bank, the goods are not paid for until you are able to negotiate that bank note and receive the money. The bank note must be proven good for actual money and that actual money handed over to you. If you own a home with a mortgage, you have a lien (hypothecation) on your property by the lender.

Thus, all of the unpaid goods in the merchant's (buyer's) possession belong to you until they are paid for. In addition, if the merchant sells those things that you sold him, the lien follows those things to the next person who buys them, no matter how many times they are sold, until eventually they are paid for. By the **mark** of hypothecation, you have the power to reclaim the liened property and sell it to satisfy your claim. The goods are not physically marked. They are legally marked. This is accomplished by what is known as an "Operation of law."

> *"**Operation of law** – This term expresses the manner in which rights, and sometimes liabilities, devolve upon a person by the mere application to the particular transaction of the established rules of law, <u>without the act or co-operation</u> of the party himself. Black's Law Dictionary, 6th Ed."*

To example the "Operation of law,""When one fails to make his house payment for three months in a row, he is not necessarily informed that he has been in default. The default is not a physical mark, but it is an **operation of law.** By operation of law, the lender now has the right to pursue a foreclosure. The final **operation of law** is to have you removed from the premises, and, without any cooperation from you.

Now use your house with the mortgage on it as an example. Imagine you are able to sell your house and you did not pay the lender (mortgage) off at the sale. The lender's lien would then remain attached to the property. The new buyer would be making payments to his lender. The original lien from your lender would continue to be attached to the property no matter how many times it was sold until that final date when the lien was paid in its entirety.

Liens don't occur in the common law in the normal transactions of buying or selling. One may get a common law lien through a court judgment, but that is not what we are referring to concerning the liens placed upon goods not paid for. In the common law the sale is immediately extinguished with actual payment of substance. The liens we are concerned with in this book only occur in commercial transactions.

Chapter 8

Common Law and Rights

"Is life so dear, or peace so sweet, as to be purchased at the price of chains and slavery? Forbid it Almighty God! I know not what course others may take, but as for me, give me liberty or give me death!"
(Patrick Henry, Founding Father)

Common law is the law of the land – the rules by which people must live with each other honorably. As mentioned, you have the absolute right to own and defend yourself, family and property. As you were forbidden to steal, theft against you, even by the state, was forbidden. You were entitled to a fair trial by your peers. Testimony had to be honest. Bearing false witness (perjury) was a serious crime. At least two people had to testify against you. You had the right to face your accuser. An accuser could not be a fiction (artificial creation like a corporation, agency, board, bureau, office, department, commission, county, state, etc.) but had to be the actual injured party, a man or woman. And most importantly, you had the right to present all relevant facts to the jury of your peers. You determined the relevance of the facts of the case - whatever you thought pertinent to the incident.

These rights were enshrined in the great charter of English liberty called the Magna Charta, mentioned previously.

The law of the land was mentioned many times as protection of the freemen. Note provision 39 of the Great Charter:

> *"No freemen shall be taken or imprisoned or disseised or exiled or in any way destroyed, nor will we go upon him nor send upon him, except by the lawful judgment of his peers or by the <u>law of the land.</u>"* (Emphasis added)

In other words, no one, including the state, could harm anyone in any way except by lawful (common law) judgment of his peers or by the law of the land. Yes, the law of the land permits a man to shoot you dead on the spot without waiting for the judgment of your peers should you break into his home or rape his wife.

Common Law gave you Rights and Liberties. It gave you the absolute right to own property. In the common law, all rights arise from property. Why? Go back to the section on debt. If you are a debtor and have no property, you are at the mercy of your creditor. A contract requires that you have substance to offer in the exchange. Hence, you must have unliened property of some kind to contract. If your property is encumbered, you are not sovereign. You are subject to the creditor. Your "right" to contract then becomes a mere privilege granted by the creditor.

The common law gives you the absolute right to lawfully contract without any interference from the government.

We use the term "lawfully" since you could not contract to violate the common law, such as to kill someone. You were free to do anything at all, provided that you did not trespass on others' Rights and Liberties! After all, is not free will a blessing?

Chapter 9

A Primer on the Creation of our Nation

"A little revolution now and then is a good thing; the tree of liberty must be refreshed from time to time with the blood of patriots and tyrants."
(Thomas Jefferson, 3rd U.S. President)

The American concept of the source of power was unique in the world. Unlike the government of kingdoms, in our nation, rights came from a single God or Creator. In accordance with this concept we were created with *free will* and unalienable rights, which came through and from the common law. The word unalienable means that which cannot be liened or separated from you. These rights cannot be taken from you by force. You cannot even voluntarily relinquish them. You cannot in any way surrender or lose an unalienable right. Bouvier's Law Dictionary:

> **UNALIENABLE.** *The state of a thing or right which cannot be sold.*

These rights were carried forth as our birthright in the common law of England. The common law was not a written law, but custom handed down for generations. Our founders were not ignorant of the Magna Charta. Its liberties were brought forward into the Constitution. But the flow of power and Sovereignty in the American Republic is important.

In the Treaty of Paris of 1783, King George surrendered his power to the People. A landmark Supreme Court case stated that the People became kings (sovereigns) without subjects. A king can make compacts (contracts) with other kings (sovereigns).

> *"…at the revolution, the sovereignty devolved on the people; and they are truly the sovereigns of the country, but they are sovereigns without subjects (unless the African [472] slaves among us may be so called) and have none to govern but themselves; the citizens of America are equal as fellow citizens, and as joint tenants in the sovereignty."* Chisholm v. Georgia (February Term, 1793) 2 U.S. (2 Dall.) 419, 1 L.Ed 440.

The chain of authority flowed as follows: Creator → Man (kings) → state → United States. Historically, the Creator endowed us with unalienable rights. These included but were not limited to the right to Life, Liberty, the Pursuit of Happiness, to contract, and to own property.

We, the People created the several states from our Common Law, the Law of Immemorial Antiquity, which is also known as the Rule of Law. We endowed the states with powers we had from the common law to protect us. We could not grant the state any power that we did not possess!

Examples: Each of us does not have the right to take money from one's neighbor and give that money to another. That is not within our *inherent* rights. Hence, we then cannot delegate such a right that we did not originally have to the state. Therefore, the state cannot take money from one's neighbor to give it to another.

Further, within our unalienable rights, none have the right to _license_ his neighbor in any of his talents (from the Creator) that he uses to make a living or otherwise. We, each of us, do not have such a right as that. Therefore, we cannot delegate such a power to the state that we, ourselves, did not have within our unalienable rights from the Creator!

Moreover, none of us can compel our neighbors to buy insurance to cover our personal losses. That simply is not a right inherent in each of us. Thus, the state cannot, by delegation from the People, have such a right to compel us to insure each other's losses. That is simply because that kind of authority cannot be traced back to a delegated grant from the People found within their inherent rights.

What needs your paramount attention are the fictions of laws such as corporations, limited liability companies, partnerships, etc. I cannot create a fiction to control my neighbor, nor to control you. No natural right is given to any of us to create a fiction within our common law. For this reason, such a delegation of power cannot be granted from the People to our states under our natural rights. It simply does not exist, because it cannot be traced back to us. Hence, corporations cannot be created by the states to control the citizens within it. Yet currently every aspect of our lives is controlled by a myriad of corporations and/or agencies on a daily basis in defiance of *common law*.

The state is created under the fundamental principles of our Common Law instruments (the state constitutions). The constitutions cannot expand, add to, create, usurp, or empower itself of any authority that specifically cannot be traced to a natural and unalienable (inherent) right that is in both you and me. We can only delegate inherent rights to the state for our protection. Unlawful (un "common law") expansions are a violation of the fundamental principles upon which each state's constitution was adopted.

The Declaration of Independence memorializes these facts explicitly. It states that people institute government to protect their rights. That is the stated purpose of a People-created government.

Since all powers granted to government come from the people within their common law rights, power absent from the people cannot be delegated to the government. The people formed the states for their protection. Following the Revolutionary War, the states became free and independent, and not only of Great Britain. They were free and independent unto themselves as well. Knowing European history, they had rightful fears that there could be disputes among them. They were well familiar with economic wars, strife, and even violent wars. In order to better preserve peace, prosperity and tranquility, the states formed a new entity called the United States to supervise their international affairs. That included affairs among the several states, and affairs between a state(s) and a foreign nation.

The states redelegated very limited powers that the People had given to the states to the national government. The original compact among the states was the Articles of Confederation. After the war, the people were dearly afraid of too much centralized power. The articles were a compact to prevent war among the states, provide for common defense and foster trade and commerce with universally accepted weights and measures for money.

The articles included some important terms that few people know. They recognized more than one status of a man.

> "...the free inhabitants of each of these States, paupers, vagabonds, and fugitives from justice excepted, shall be entitled to all privileges and immunities of free citizens in the several States" (Article IV)

This is important. One could be a "free inhabitant" which is clearly distinguished from "free citizen." This certainly fits the quote from Chisholm vs. Georgia, page 32. If you are a sovereign, you are unto yourself only, free of ties of the state, except those ties you freely enter. We will see proof of that in the next chapter when we discuss citizenship a bit more.

The articles fell short in one area, namely raising revenue to support the new central government. So, the states reconvened in the Constitutional convention to draft a new compact. Taxing powers were written in among the other powers such as regulating commerce among the states, international commerce, defense, post offices, etc. These powers were still strictly limited. The United States got exclusive jurisdiction over the District of Columbia and lands it exclusively owned (Territories).

The United States had no jurisdiction or power over the people or inhabitants within the states (Baron vs. Baltimore[1]). Men and women owed their allegiance to their state, which afforded them their legal protection and rem-

---

[1] **Barron vs. Baltimore (1833)** – John Barron was co-owner of a profitable wharf in the harbor of Baltimore. As the city developed and expanded, large amounts of sand accumulated in the harbor, depriving Barron of the deep waters, which had been the key to his successful business. He sued the city to recover a portion of his financial losses.
- Issue: Does the Fifth Amendment deny the states as well as the national government the right to take private property for public use without justly compensating the property's owner?
- Decision: The Court announced its decision in this case without even hearing the arguments of the City of Baltimore. Writing for the unanimous Court, Chief Justice Marshall found that the limitations on government articulated in the **Fifth Amendment** were specifically **intended to limit the powers of the national government.** Citing the intent of the framers and the development of the Bill of Rights as an exclusive check on the government in Washington D.C., Marshall argued that the Supreme Court had no jurisdiction in this case since the Fifth Amendment was not applicable to the states.
- effect: the **Bill of Rights applies only to the national government, not the states.** Between 1880 and 1924, the Court rejected incorporation in 9 occasions, and stuck by the Barron rule. (This means that this case was an example of non-incorporation of the people of the states into the Constitution.)

edies in law. Powers the people did not have could not be delegated to the state. And powers not delegated to the states by their People could not be re-delegated to the United States, since the states did not get those powers to begin with from the people.

Chapter 10

I know of no safe depository of the ultimate powers of the society but the people themselves; and if we think them not enlightened enough to exercise their control with wholesome discretion, the remedy is not to take it from them, but to inform their discretion by education. This is the true corrective of abuses of constitutional power.
(Thomas Jefferson, 3rd U.S. President)

In opening this chapter we are compelled to remind you that it was not the People who ordained the constitution as is commonly taught in schools and near universally believed because of the Preamble "**We the People….**". We again elaborate directly from The Encyclopedia of the American Constitution, copyright 1986, by Macmillan Publishing Company, A Division of Macmillan, In. 866 Third Avenue, New York, NY 10022 Page 367 CONSTITUTIONAL HISTORY before 1776:

> "The opening words of the United States Constitution, "We the People," startled some of the old revolutionaries of 1776. Patrick Henry, after expressing the highest veneration for the men who wrote the words, demanded "What right had they to say, "We the People.""

"... Who authorized them to speak the language of **We, the People***, instead of We, the States?" It was a good question and, as Henry knew, not really answerable. No one had authorized the members of the Constitutional Convention to speak for the People of the United States. They had been chosen by the legislatures of thirteen sovereign states and were authorized only to act for the governments of those states in redefining the relationships among them. Instead, they had dared not only to act for "the People of the United States" but also to proclaim what they did as "the supreme law of the land," supreme apparently over the actions of the existing state governments and supreme also over the government that the Constitution itself would create for the United States."*

This is most revealing in the structure of power. It was the sovereign states and NOT the People that ordained the new Constitution. Next we look at the new entity called "United States".

Now what was this entity called the United States? You might be surprised to learn that it was deemed a ***corporation*** in a Supreme Court case:

"The United States of America are a **corporation** *endowed with the capacity to sue and be sued, to convey and receive property."* 1 Marsh. Dec. 177, 181.

"The United States Government is a foreign **corporation** *with respect to a state."* Volume 20: Corpus

Juris Sec. §1785: NY re: Merriam 36 N.E. 505 1441 S.Ct.1973, 41 L.Ed.287

Its primary power was to regulate commerce. Please indulge our elaboration. What is commerce? [2] (Please read the Footnote). It is the movement of goods through <u>navigation</u> across fictional international borders for resale. It is not, nor ever was, the private affairs of private people transacting among themselves. Trade amongst and between people is their unalienable right. The states at the time were sovereign and independent. Court cases confirm that they were foreign to each other. They were literally free and independent separate nations that entered into a commercial and defense compact with each other. Originally, they accomplished that end through the Articles of Confederation. These articles were weak in that they did not provide sufficient means to raise revenue for the central government. The states then convened to create the

---

2 The following is a quote from "Lex Mercatoria" A Complete Code of Commercial Law – Originally published: 6th ed. 1795

AN HISTORICAL DEDUCTION OF TRADE AND COMMERCE, FROM THEIR ORIGIN

Quoted from the third paragraph under the above heading: "Commerce is that intercourse with foreign nations, which is carried on from one country to another *by means of navigation*; either for the exchange of commodities, or for the sale or purchase of them, through the medium of money. *Commerce then, has its basis in navigation*, and is supported by Exports and Imports, whereas simple trade may be transacted independent of these elements and commerce, and herein chiefly consists the difference."

NAVIGATION – Is the art of sailing at sea, also the manner of trading: and a navigator is one who understands *Navigation*, or imports goods in foreign bottoms. Page 356 Lex Mercatoria, 1795

Constitution with greater taxing powers over commerce. Their agent was the corporate United States.

We will now show you how you have been placed, through shenanigans, into commerce. You have been fraudulently placed into commerce so that the U.S. Government can use its supreme power (to regulate commerce) to regulate you and everything you do on the land.

The footnote tells you more of commerce. But more obvious proof is the following. If you hold a commercial license and drive a truck for a living, you deliver a "Bill of Lading" along with the *cargo* in the back of your big rig. What jurisdiction (law) are you traveling within? Your commercial license implies you are in commerce. But what places you in commerce? Note the definitions of a Bill of Lading and a Way Bill from the Law Dictionary of Bouvier:

> (**In footnote 2 (page 41),** *there could be no more accurate definitions of the meanings of the words used in the constitution than the Lex Mercatoria, published in 1795, for this was their rule in those days.*)

> **BILL OF LADING,** *contracts and commercial law. A memorandum or acknowledgment in writing, signed by the captain or master of a ship or other vessel, that he has <u>received in good order, on board of his ship or vessel</u>, therein named, at the place therein mentioned, certain goods therein specified, which he promises to deliver in like good order, (the dangers of the seas excepted,) at the place therein appointed for the delivery*

> *of the same, to the consignee therein named or to his*
> *assigns, he or they paying freight for the same. 1 T. R.*
> *745; Bac. Abr. Merchant L Com. Dig. Merchant E 8. b;*
> *Abbott on Ship. 216 1 Marsh. on Ins.*

As is clearly evident, the **Bill of Lading** is a list of goods that a captain of a ship signs for, and then navigates those goods over the sea to a destination. The question is, "Why are truck drivers carrying Bills of Lading when plainly by our own observations they travel on the land?"

However, just so one does not mistake that the *Bill of Lading* is perhaps a kind of Bill that may be used for *land as well as sea*, let us look at the Bill for goods transported over land, the *"Way Bill"*, which is defined by Bouvier's Law Dictionary.

> **WAY BILL**, *contracts. A writing in which is set down*
> *the names of passengers, who are carried in a public*
> *conveyance, or the description of goods sent with a*
> *common carrier by land; when the goods are carried*
> *by water, the instrument is called a bill of lading. (q.v.)*
> *Defined from Bouvier's Law Dictionary*

You may now state, "Oh, this is just plain silly! It is just an error for truckers, who are in commerce, to use the Bill of Lading." But consider this, when the big rigs reach their destinations they back their big rigs into the "bay" and up to the loading "dock" of a store, building etc. And yet, the stores or buildings are on the land. If you don't believe it, ask a trucker.

Now, "What about you?" Could you be in commerce (traveling on the sea) when you are traveling in your automobile? We ask you this, "Have you ever passed raised or painted islands that were in the middle of the road? Of course you have. The law states that it is a violation of law, or forbidden for you to drive over the island. Think about ships, can they maneuver over islands? No, they can't. Why the use of the term "island" when clearly you can only drive on the land? Also, do you often have a passenger in your vehicle? Black's Law Dictionary defines passenger as follows:

> **PASSENGER** – *One carried for hire, or reward, as distinguished from a "guest" who is one carried gratuitously, that is, without any financial return except such slight benefit as is customary as part of the ordinary courtesy of the road. Duncan v. Hutchinson, 139 Ohio St. 185, 39 N.E.2d 140, 142.*

As you know, the traffic laws titles those, other than the driver, as passengers and not guests. When you are driving do those, who are traveling with you, fit the term passenger or guest? Again, the law deems them to be passengers, though they are most certainly guests as defined above.

We know if you have been driving for a length of time, you have stopped at a gas station or hundreds of stations over the course of your life. Do you know what a station is? Let's define it by Bouvier's Law Dictionary**:**

> **STATION**, *civil law. A place where ships may ride in safety. Dig. 49, 12, 1, 13; id. 50, 15, 59.*

Certainly, the term **station** applies to the sea, but, the Lex Mercatoria stated that commerce applied to the **navigation of the sea**. It must be impossible to jump to the conclusion that your automobile is a ship or vessel on the sea, or is it? (See "vessel" in image at end of chapter, page *59*.)

In the United State there has been a War on Drugs for at least 30–40 years. These laws make it illegal to have drug paraphernalia, which is by law defined as **contraband.** (Reference: Wikipedia) "Drug paraphernalia is defined by the American federal Drug Enforcement Administration as any equipment, product, or material that is modified for making, using, or concealing illegal drugs such as cocaine, heroin, marijuana, and methamphetamine, those items used with a <u>drug</u>." Do you know precisely what contraband is? Do you know under what *law* the word 'contraband' falls? Does it fall within the Common law, Equity law (contract), or Admiralty (the law of the sea), which includes Maritime?

Let's see how the term contraband is used in a time of *war*. The following is from Bouvier:

> *[**Note**, the word after CAPTURE below is the word **war**. Hence, the word capture falls exclusively within the theater of war.]*

> ***CAPTURE***, *war. The taking of property by one belligerent from another.*
> *2. To make a good capture of a ship, it must be subdued and taken by an enemy in open war, or by way*

of reprisals, or by a pirate, and with intent to deprive the owner of it.

*3. Capture may be with intent to possess both ship and cargo, or only to seize the goods of the enemy, or **contraband goods**, which are on board:*

So, it is easily seen how the term contraband is used in a time of war. But what law does it fall under? The Common Law? The Equity Law? Or, the Admiralty/Maritime Law?

Here is how Bouvier Law Dictionary defines the term **contraband**:

> [**Note**, the two words after *CONTRABAND* below stands for **"Maritime Law"**. Hence, the term contraband falls within the Admiralty/Maritime authority on the seas."]

> **CONTRABAND**, mar. law. Its most extensive sense, means all **_commerce_** which is carried on contrary to the laws of the state. This term is also used to designate all kinds of merchandise, which are used, or transported, against the interdictions published by a ban or solemn cry.

> 2. The term is usually applied to that **_unlawful commerce_** which **_is so carried on in time of war._** Merlin, Repert. h.t. **Commodities particularly useful in war are contraband as arms, ammunition, horses, timber for ship building, and every kind of naval stores.**

> *3. **Contraband of war**, is the act by which, in times of war, a neutral vessel introduces, or attempts to introduce into the territory of, one of the belligerent parties, arms, ammunition, or other effects intended for, or which may serve, hostile operations. Merlin, Repert. h.t. 1 Kent, Com. 135; Mann. Comm. B. 3, c. 7; 6 Mass. 102; 1 Wheat. 382; 1 Cowen, 56 John. Cas. 77, 120.*

From the above defining of the term *contraband*, it should be clear that *contraband* only arises within the *law of the sea*. Yet, everyday, in every state, people are arrested for having contraband within their automobiles. Make any sense to you?

Next time you go to register a vehicle with the Department of Motor Vehicles, look at the top of the form. It reads "Vehicle/Vessel". Isn't it a policy that when one uses the "/" between words that they have similar meaning, or fall within the same use? We specifically draw your attention to the fact that the term Vessel is used by the DMV. (See Page 59) Why do you think they place that term on DMV documents?

The Congress of the United States has the delegated power to regulate any continuous line/lane. So if it is continuous, or what is deemed, "effectively connected" to a continuous line/lane, the U.S. Congress (or the state) has supreme authority over it. To name a few *lines* or *lanes* that the reader knows for sure the Congress (or state) has the right to regulate: Airlines, train lines, bus lines, cable car lines, telegraph lines, telephone lines, shipping lanes, and the beat goes on…. But there are probably lines/lanes you have not thought of, such as: gas lines, sewer lines, water lines, electrical lines (the grid), transmitter lines, such as radio or television, inclusive of cable lines and the Internet. As is clearly evident, the Congress of the U.S. has control over most every thing that is in commerce or that affects the commerce in any way. That would include such things as a strike of the employees of any of the previous major named lines.

We had mentioned sewer lines above. Unless one is on a septic tank, the toilet is attached to the sewer line. In commerce, that would constitute a "station" as defined above. Also, the one using the appliance is deemed, "effectively connected." That would include standing over the commode with a continuous stream touching the water within the device. Each flush enters the line, and is regulated by the delegated grant of power to regulate commerce. And, you presumed you were on the land? Do not forget the water from the tap, and also the drain, are both in commerce. And, as you are using the water, the actions are effectively connected to commerce. (Your electrical power arrives through commercial lines as well affixing your house to commerce.) Certainly, and as you may have understood by the Lex Mercatoria's definition of the word "commerce" (See the Second Footnote), anything related to the navigation on the seas or *effectively connected* to the navigation on the sea, is in commerce. These aspects of commerce, which have been just explained, are an essential aspect supporting "𝕿𝖍𝖊𝖞 **Own It All (Including You!)**". They, however, in and of themselves are not the mark.

Have you, while traveling on the highways of the United States, noticed the signs that have a shield shaped symbol designating the number of the highway? Such as U.S. Highway Route 101, the famous Route 66, and on? The shape is distinctly similar to an officer's badge. Obviously, these are U.S. or United States highways. And, are they not continuous lanes? Of course they are. It is a fact that continuous lanes and lines are within the delegated grants to Congress to regulate the same when they cross state territorial *lines*. We or most of us have heard of shipping lanes on the high seas. Have you thought about the highways as shipping lanes? Well, they are. Note the big rigs carrying their cargo, and having the Bill of Ladings, which is defined for the goods on board ship. Again, ask a trucker about the bay and the loading dock, and note the raised and painted islands, as you change *lanes*. Are they not regulated? Well, regulations are not the law of the land, but the law of the seas under the power of Congress (or the state) to regulate commerce.

Further, in the early '50's, the State of California enacted a law. The law *renamed* all streets, boulevards, avenues, and etc., except cul-de-sacs (where the roads stop), to highways. And of course, this act did not actually change those names currently applied to the roads. But nonetheless, all of these roads became highways, and are effectively connected to the U.S. highways. Are you able to visualize what this means? All highways that are effectively connected to the U.S. highways are within the control of the Congress of the United States. Moreover, all U.S. Highways are shipping lanes; hence, attachment to the same Congressional jurisdiction. That includes such streets (now a highway) where you reside. It has become a shipping lane. Have you seen buses, cars, trucks, etc. on your street? They all are on shipping lanes.

Now imagine all of those shipping lanes throughout the United States. Also note that these shipping lanes in major cities surround blocks of land, and in the country large portions of land. What 'term' defines a mass of land surrounded by water? If you haven't figured it out, ask a third grader (are you smarter???), for the answer because that certainly is a test question for him. Next question is, "When you enter one of those areas surrounded by water, what is that place of entry called? A port? Yes, a port. Could it also be a *haven*? Bouvier defines "haven" as follows:

> **HAVEN**. *A place calculated for the reception of ships, and so situated, in regard to the surrounding land, that the vessel may ride at anchor in it in safety. Hale,*

de Port. Mar. c. 2; 2 Chit. Com. Law, 2; 15 East, R. 304, 5. Vide Creek; Port; Road.

Well, did you replenish your *vessel* at the *station*; purchased your *cargo* from the *market*; acted as a *carrier* for *passengers*; maneuvered upon the *shipping lanes* within the *highways*? Did you have a destination for *home port/haven*, which is a mass of land surrounded by shipping lanes? Does your homeport have an entrance called a driveway, which is effectively connected to the highway upon which shipping lanes exist; and did you place your vessel under a car**port**? Before you reached your homeport did you take the highway to the Postal Service, and do business? Upon leaving the Postal Service did you read the lettering on the glass doors, which states, "Thank you for **shipping** with us? And, did not the Postal Service **ship** the item you gave across town, country, or internationally by first using the shipping lanes, and then air lanes?

 Are you curious to know under which law, Common, Equity, or Admiralty, the "naturalization"[3] clause for aliens to become citizens of the United States falls? We believe you should know this because it is of paramount importance and relevancy to all of your activities. In the Lex Mercatoria (1795), page 368 you will find naturalization defined. It is in the Code of Commercial Law, or the Admiralty/Maritime jurisdiction. If that last sentence was not clear, then stated clearly, ***"Naturalization falls under and is subject to the Maritime Jurisdiction of the United States".***

---

3   Naturalization is the means by which an alien, one from a foreign country, may become a United States Citizen under the 14th Amendment to the United States Constitution.

Check out the 14th Amendment of the United States Constitution to view the term naturalization below. When an alien has lived on the land for a certain amount of time, learnt the language, and studied the history, he may move in the Maritime Jurisdiction [the law of the Sea] of the United States to apply for naturalization. Interesting? He appears to be on the land while moving about, yet he legally moves by the law of the Sea to become naturalized. Ah, but you state that these aliens cross the sea to get here, so they are connected to the law of the sea. Then, what of the Canadian and the Mexican? Neither has to arrive by sea!

The 14th Amendment to the United States Constitution Section 1:

> **Section 1.** *All **persons born or naturalized** in the United States, and subject to the jurisdiction thereof, **are citizens of the United States** and of the State wherein they reside. No State shall make or enforce any law which shall abridge the **privileges or immunities** of citizens of the United States; nor shall any State deprive any person of life, liberty, or property, without due process of law; nor deny to any person within its jurisdiction the equal protection of the laws.*

The most important point one needs to learn from the first section of the 14th Amendment is that those born here and subject to the jurisdiction thereof, and those naturalized and subject to the jurisdiction thereof, are both citizens of the United States. Further, they have the same privileges and immunities. **(Not Rights!)** They are on equal footing to each other, and receive exactly the same protection (privileges and immunities), whether born here or naturalized.

Concerning this section 1 of the 14th Amendment let's look at a principle of law that Jesus stated: "Know a tree by the fruit it bares." Stated clearly, if one came upon a tree that had oranges hanging from its limbs, Jesus states that the tree is an orange tree. Now, visualize the tree as Maritime law. Thousands of aliens dangle from its limbs as new citizens of the United States. Again, Maritime is the law of the sea. And if the law of the sea "*bares*" (creates) the status of "citizen of the United States", then the citizen arises out of the law of navigation (again, see footnote 2, page 41) on the high sea. Created under commerce, he, "the citizen", would be automatically under the control of the Maritime/commerce (Admiralty in time of emergency) jurisdiction. That's simply another way of saying that he would be "subject to the jurisdiction thereof."

But what about those who were not aliens and are citizens of the United States by being born here? We quote from section one again, "...born or naturalized...are citizens of the United States." This amendment has made the status of being born here equivalent to being naturalized. There is no difference in the eyes of the "corporate" United States in either. Friend, you too are dangling from the limbs of the tree of Maritime law. The status of a "citizen of the United States" was created within the Maritime jurisdiction. If you are born in the United States, and find your way into its jurisdiction, you are a subject of the Maritime jurisdiction, on equal footing with the naturalized alien. We'll state this another way. We have shown you that the United States is a corporation (page 40). Hence, if you are a "citizen of the United States," you have taken your rights (privileges and immunities) from a corporation in commerce, rather than receiving unalienable Rights from the Creator. How's that make you feel? Has your reality changed? The pertinent question is, "Will you help shift the reality to the land?" In subsequent chapters we will show you how you have absolutely entered into the commercial authority of the United States, making yourself a "citizen of the United States""subject" to its jurisdiction (authority). And now the distinction between "citizen" and inhabitant becomes much clearer. A citizen has entered into a compact with the governmental corporation, or come under its sphere of authority. The inhabitant or "Sovereign" (*See* Chisholm vs. Georgia, Chapter 9) has not so entangled himself with the government corporation.

Without getting too deeply into this subject of citizenship, it is important to know what brought about the passage of the 14th Amendment. The "citizenship" was created for the newly freed black slaves. Black slaves were considered commercial property of their master. And additionally, they had a direct commercial tax upon them imposed by the United States Government. For every black slave imported into this country, the master had to pay a ten-dollar tax upon each head. The slaves remained the commercial property of their masters until the end of the Civil War. They then were commercial property of the victorious government. Now we ask you in the light of the Maritime tree that bares fruit, "Were the slaves ever really freed?" The 14th Amendment merely granted "privileges and immunities" under the tree of Admiralty/Maritime rather than the unalienable Rights white people inherently had within the common law. But that wasn't enough for the corporate United States. The 14th amendment provided a trick means to pull the entire population under the umbrella of that same commercial jurisdiction, stripping unalienable Rights equally from all. You will soon discover how the entire population was moved into commerce. Then, all Americans were granted *statutory* civil rights, privileges and immunities from the corporate government, rather than possessing the Sovereign and unalienable Rights the Creator endowed them with.

What if we could, by fraud, get you to believe that certain words, like *passenger*, *pass book*, *contraband*, and *station* actually belong to the law of the land. And then by your use and actions upon those words we applied the Law of the Sea over you. Would we be the Ultimate Beguiler? The United States has never adopted the Law of the Land (See next paragraph for case law). Your common law, from which your unalienable rights arise, comes from the Creator. The U.S. moves within the Admiralty jurisdiction (actions with penalties). Further, all the states have done away with common law crimes (witness California):

> *"There are no common law crimes in California; i.e., no act or omission is criminal, except as prescribed by the Penal Code, or other statute, ordinance, or municipal, county, or township regulation." (P.C. 6; see In re harder*

> *(1935) 9 C.A.2d 153, 155, 49 P.2d 304; People v. Harris (1961) 191 C.A.2d 754, 758, 12 C.R. 916; Keeler v. Superior Court (1970) 2 C.3d 619, 631, 87 C.R. 481, 470 P.2d 617; **for similar rule in other states**, see 21 Am.Jur.2d, Criminal Law § 7; Perkins 3d, p. 38; 1 Wharton, Crim. Law § 9; for same rule as to crimes against the United States, see United States v. Eaton (1892) 144 U.S. 677, 12 S.Ct. 764, 36 L.Ed. 591; Perkins 3d, p. 37; 1 Wharton, Crim. Law § 9.) But the common law may properly be looked to for the meaning of words in a criminal statute.*

Heck, while we are at it, we'll prove that there are not any common law crimes against the United States either:

> *"It is well settled that there are no common-law offenses against the United States." U.S. v. Hudson, 7 Cranch, 32; U. S. v. Coolidge, 1 Wheat. 415; U. S. v. Britton, 108 U.S. 199, 206, 2 S. Sup. Ct. Rep. 531; Manchester v. Massachusetts, 139 U.S. 240, 262, 263 S., 11 Sup. Ct. Rep. 559, and cases there cited.*

Well, if there are no common law crimes in either the state or federal jurisdictions, then what other jurisdiction allows a penalty for a crime? Admiralty jurisdiction, and none other! We hope that by now we have driven home the point through and through.

Want further proof? Just go to Article 3 of the Constitution. That's the article that set up the judicial branch. Only three jurisdictions are granted to the courts: Admiralty/Maritime (international contract), equity (the law of contract), and

Law. Law meant common law. However, the United States never adopted common law (United States v. Hudson, 7 Cranch (U.S.) 32; United States v Coolidge, 1 Wheat. (U.S.) 415). The United States only retained jurisdiction over Equity and Admiralty/Maritime in federal courts. If the courts had no other jurisdiction, then the central government wielded no other powers.

Why did the federal government not adopt the common law? There was no need. The United States had no jurisdiction over the people of the states who were within the common law. You'll see that in the 9th and 10th amendments. All powers not granted to central government were reserved to the people and their states. Those powers are their common law rights.

Restraints against the Federal government from attacking their common law rights are found in the first 8 amendments. (See below quote) While these are known as the Bill of Rights, this is a misnomer. Rights came from the Creator, not the Constitution. Those amendments were really a Bill of Restraints against the Federal government from ever moving on those common law rights. Don't believe us? Here is the Preamble to the "Bill of Rights".

> *"THE Conventions of a number of the States having at the time of their adopting the Constitution, expressed a desire, in order to prevent misconstruction or abuse of its powers, that further declaratory and **restrictive clauses** should be added: And as extending the ground of public confidence in the Government, will best insure the beneficent ends of its institution…"*

57

The preamble clearly states that the amendments are restrictions (See footnote 1, page 36) against the central government. The amendments were not a declaration of rights the people already possessed! Rights *never* did come from the constitution. Rights are inherent in man.

Let's look closer at other specific powers granted the central government. The states were interested in fair trade and commerce, both for the sake of the common law people on the land and for external commerce. To foster this, the central government was constitutionally granted the power to coin money via a uniform standard of weights and measures. Money was defined as gold and silver coin, right out of the common law. With this power, Congress passed the Coinage Act of 1792. It provided for specific weights of coined gold or silver as lawful (common law) money. Weighed and impressed with the seal of the government, it would be harder to cheat someone.

Now remember Article 3 of the Constitution. It created the judicial branch, called the Supreme Court. Congress also created lower courts called "District Courts of the United States." You'll be interested to know that the Coinage Act mandated the money of accounts of these courts to be the gold and silver coin authorized by the Act. (See Appendix F) Can you now see the scales of Solomon? Real Courts of the United States were backed by real coin (substance) weighed and measured and **seal**ed by the United States. Seal, as stated, is literally the CERTIFICATION by the U.S. of the substance in relation to the stated value.

The business of the United States was commerce. Commerce at that time did eventually require gold in payment of debt. That's what the bills of exchange were all about. The United States was a commercial overseer of international transactions. It was not a People overseer. The effect of the 14th amendment was to place a new ruler over formerly free and independent people, effectively reinstating the king (the corporate United States) over your Sovereign self. However, even citizens of the United States still enjoyed the "right" to property. And with property rights, they still retained very significant control over their lives. So just how did the central government acquire power to regulate or invade just about every aspect of the lives of everyone, regardless of race? Read on in the book.

Below is proof that a vehicle is a vessel or that they are equivalent terms concerning how the government has incorporated these terms in this DMV form with the placement of the punctuation known as a slash in "vehicle/vessel":

DMV
A Public Service Agency

VEHICLE/VESSEL TRANSFER AND REASSIGNMENT FORM

This form is not the ownership certificate. It must accompany the titling document or application for a duplicate title.

INSTRUCTIONS ON REVERSE SIDE   ALL SIGNATURES MUST BE IN INK   PHOTOCOPIES NOT ACCEPTED

SECTION 1: Vehicle/Vessel Description

IDENTIFICATION NUMBER	YEAR MODEL	MAKE	LICENSE PLATE/CF #	MOTORCYCLE ENGINE #
WDBPA 4SA0DB024046	1983	MERZ		

SECTION 2: Bill of Sale

I/We _____ sell, transfer, and deliver the above vehicle/vessel

Allstate Insurance Company
(PRINT SELLER'S NAME(S))

to _____ on [MO DAY YR] for the amount of $ _____
(PRINT BUYER'S NAME(S))   (SELLING PRICE)

If this was a gift, indicate relationship: _____ (e.g., parents, spouse, friend, etc.) $ _____
(GIFT VALUE)

Defining the Slash "/" – from Wikipedia: [http://en.wikipedia.org/wiki/Slash_(punctuation)] "The most common use [for the slash] is to replace the <u>hyphen</u> or <u>en dash</u> to make clear a strong joint between words or phrases, such as "the Hemingway/Faulkner generation".

The following is from "WriteExpress" http://www.writeexpress.com/slash.html concerning the "/"

Slashes can also be used to designate alternative spellings or names.

Examples: Elizabeth/Beth/Betty/Liz – Civil War/War Between the States – Zeus/Jupiter

In informal writing, the slash can be used for paired terms such as on/off. Even in casual writing a slash should be used in this way only sparingly, and such constructions should generally be avoided in formal writing. When used with paired terms, the slash does not have a space before or after it. Note: Before beginning work, make sure to check the on/off valve. Well, it's not really a yes/no type of question. Unfortunately, she's known for her hot/cold personality.

CHAPTER 11

UNDER HONEST MONEY

"The colonies would gladly have borne the little tax on tea and other matters had it not been that England took away from the colonies their money, which created unemployment and dissatisfaction. The inability of the colonists to get power to issue their own money permanently out of the hands of George III and the international bankers was the PRIME reason for the Revolutionary War."
(Benjamin Franklin's autobiography)

Do you ever recall in your education reading the above direct quote from the famous Founder about the real cause of the war? Not we (the authors) but Franklin himself tells us that the real reason was not a tax on tea. Not a tax on stamps. It was over the (dishonest) money system in the hands of the king and his banker financiers. Why do you suppose you were never taught this most fundamental root cause of the revolution? Please read on......

Under the honest system of weights and measures, the United States of America prospered greatly. Its treasury was the gold and silver of the common law. Its coin was stamped "in God we trust." The Ten Commandments were permitted and displayed in courts. People rose when God, represented by the Bible, entered the court, not when the black robed judge walked in. America became, undisputedly, the richest and most powerful nation on earth. The people worked hard. They were industrious and they righteously received the fruits of their labor.

Please review just a partial list of the unalienable Rights and Liberties we once had that are actually listed in the Constitution:

Contract, Speech, Press, Petition for redress of grievance, assembly, religion, weapons, security in their homes, protection from searches and seizures, protection from self incrimination, due process, protection against eminent domain property confiscation, fair trial, to be told of the nature of the crime and cause of accusation, of government taking property without just compensation to owner, cruel and unusual punishment.

Also note that nowhere in that same Constitution was provision for the central government to have the power to regulate healers, trades, professions, or to require or issue licenses to anyone not doing commerce among the states or foreign nations and Indian tribes. Nowhere did the central government have the power to restrict travel or personal liberty with licenses. Nowhere did the central government have any power over the people within the states, unless they were operating in **navigable** commerce. (Lex Merc.)

Here's your proof.

Most people think that our rights come from the "Bill of Rights," instead of from our Creator. The Bill of Rights was meant to be restrictions against the U.S. Central Government.

In the Supreme Court case called Baron vs. Baltimore (page 36), the court held that the 1st eight amendments (the so called Bill of Rights) did not pertain to the people of the States. Why? They were never subject to the jurisdiction of the United States central government. If they were subject to central government powers, the amendments would have had to be applicable to them to provide protection against governmental abuses. The amendments would be needed to balance out whatever invasive powers the central government might have had.

The Supreme Court has repeatedly told us how the Bill of Rights became applicable to the people of the States. It happened through the 14th amendment. This book is not going to tackle the controversies surrounding the 14th amendment. That's for another day. However, it is important to point out one thing. The 14th amendment granted the United States authority to "protect" persons subject to its jurisdiction, by imposing the restraints of the "Bill of Rights" upon the states.

http://en.wikipedia.org/wiki/Incorporation_(Bill_of_Rights)

http://en.wikipedia.org/wiki/Adamson_v._California

However, jurisdiction also means taxing power, seizures, regulations, restraints. Jurisdiction is another term for "authority over". So, it's now time to prove to you how and why you have fallen into this jurisdiction. It's time to show you that you are marked and its disastrous consequences.

Chapter 12

"In a time of universal deceit, telling the truth is a revolutionary act. (George Orwell) No generation has a right to contract debts greater than can be paid off during the course of its own existence."
(Thomas Jefferson, 3rd U.S. President)

We are going to skip ahead to 1933 for this chapter. We'll then discuss the banking system in the next and put the two together for you.

It's not our purpose to detail the forces and events leading up to the great 1933 change. It's far too political and controversial. Just make a mental note of the stock market crash of 1929, which ushered in the Great Depression. The crash occurred 16 years after the enactment of the Federal Reserve System under President Woodrow Wilson.

Until 1933, the American people transacted their trade within the common law of the land. They paid and extinguished their debts with gold or silver coin, or currency (paper instruments) redeemable in gold or silver. In early 1933, Americans realized something was wrong economically. They distrusted their government and the currency. They distrusted the pieces of paper alleging a guarantee of redemption in real substance. They began a run on the banks wanting their real money rather than notes that they questioned. Perhaps they knew that there was insufficient gold backing the numbers of gold notes in circulation. (If so, were these excess notes not issued via fraud by the government? Perhaps it was fraud on the part of bankers issuing more gold certificates than gold they had on hand? We are inclined to point the finger first at the central government since the Treasury itself was issuing gold certificates and promised redemption in writing right on the currency itself.)

The people could control their substance (gold) if in their hands. They preferred their gold, their property, rather than paper notes. Regarding paper, they had no control over it. Paper could be printed wantonly by the government or the Federal Reserve. A banking panic ensued. On March 9, 1933, newly elected President Franklin Roosevelt (FDR) declared a state of emergency (WHICH HAS NEVER BEEN LIFTED).

> *"President Franklin D. Roosevelt issued the next national emergency proclamation some 48 hours after assuming office. Proclaimed March 6, 1933, on the somewhat questionable authority of the Trading with the Enemy Act of 1917, the proclamation declared a so-called "bank holiday" and halted a major class of financial transactions by closing the banks."* Congressional Research Service, Library of Congress, Order Code 98-505 GOV National Emergency Power.

He closed the banks. Within days, two edicts were issued by the cooperation of FDR and the Congress. With a stroke of his pen, FDR signed an executive order "authorizing" the forcible confiscation of the gold coins of the American people. The people were commanded to turn in their lawful gold coins and paper certificates redeemable in gold. Not to do so subjected them to criminal penalties. This was done under the allegation that the people were "hoarding" their gold. "Hoarding" now became a crime. Now wait a minute! The gold belonged to the people that possessed it, and was their property. Retaining, saving, or otherwise holding on to their sovereign property was suddenly declared a crime. This edict only applied to U.S. Persons. <u>If you were a foreigner you could keep your gold.</u> They didn't steal from foreigners, only Americans. Now consider this. You could have been holding a gold certificate like this one:

At the top: "This certifies that there is on deposit in the Treasury of the USA".... And at the bottom: "Twenty Dollars in gold coin payable to the bearer on demand." You are the bearer of the note. Therefore you are the owner of the gold that the Treasury is holding in trust. The certificate says that the gold is payable to you. Suddenly, the USA tells you that it won't turn over your gold to you. This particular certificate also uses the word "payment" in the script on the left side. That suggests that unlike other notes, this note does represent actual payment. Actual payment is with substance, gold, which this note represents (and could be redeemed for until March 1933), as opposed to discharge. (See page 20 regarding discharge.)

This certificate is like a baggage check claim. What is the morality about someone not returning an item belonging to you? It is theft, pure and simple. It could also be that the handler became insolvent and unable to pay the debt. You know that is theft as well. And if the handler became insolvent (meaning he was unable to pay his debt) and did not reveal that fact to the holder of the claim check, it is also bearing false witness. Either the USA committed a heinous crime against the people by stealing their gold, or it was bankrupt and could not pay, and it lied, or both.

The truth is, it was both. The USA went into bankruptcy on that day. That was the basis of the emergency. They never told the American people openly. But it is in the public (Congressional) record:

> *"Mr. Speaker, we are now in chapter 11. Members of Congress are official trustees presiding over the greatest reorganization of any bankrupt entity in world history, the   U.S. Government. We are setting forth hopefully a blueprint for our future. There are some*

> *who say it is a coroner's report that will lead to our
> demise."* Congressman James Trafficant speaking.
> (Congressional Record, Vol. 139, No. 33, March 17,
> 1993)

The Congress is just a bunch of trustees for the biggest
bankruptcy in world history. It was supposed to be a reorganization. It sure was. Congress reorganized the whole
structure of America, turning it inside out. And Congress
nabbed you as security for the creditors through a horrible
scheme we will be unwrapping for you.

Is a king still a sovereign if he is in debt? How could he be?
No debtor is sovereign. He is beholden to his creditor, the
new sovereign. Who was the creditor of the USA? Hint. The
top of a financial document tells you who the creditor is.
Just look at the top of its reissued currency:

The top says "Federal Reserve Note". Also notice that this
certificate is "legal" tender. Not "lawful tender" Could this
have been the work of a trickster to beguile? Legal means
form. Lawful means both form and substance. An example

of what is meant by legal versus lawful would be: A picture of you is your form, and the actual you is both your form and substance. What you see in the mirror is form. You are both form and substance. Finally, what happened to the word "payment"?

But it gets far worse. On June 5, 1933, Congress passed HJR-192. House Joint Resolution 192 was passed to suspend the gold standard. This terminated the gold clause in the national constitution. Where did they get that authority?

The resolution specifically declared that payment in gold or a particular kind of coin or currency (gold backed) or in an amount of money measured (weighed) by the United States, now violates the "public policy." Where did the government get that authority?

(Remember, the government and Congress were only to have enumerated powers delegated by the Constitution. There is nowhere in the Constitution that granted the authority to wipe out the gold standard. Would you agree that what the Congress did was unconstitutional?) No longer could any citizen lawfully pay a debt. His means to pay debt was stolen by a "re-organized" government that was newly created. Suddenly the servant (government) became the thief or agent for another thief. (Would you agree that this, too, was unconstitutional?)

But Congress went one step further. It declared that Federal Reserve Notes shall be legal tender for all debts, public and private. It declared that every obligation anyone entered into before or following would be *discharged* (not paid) with these legal tender notes. *House Joint Resolution 192, 73d Congress, Sess. I, Ch. 48, June 5, 1933 (Public Law No. 10)*. (And would you agree that the power to do this, as well, is nowhere to be found in the Constitution unless perhaps Congress had decided that its power to **regulate** commerce gave it dictatorial power over us?)

That's why you see the word "payment" dropped from subsequent currency. We know that a debt discharged is a debt not paid. A Minnesota Supreme Court (Stanek v. White, 215 NWR 781 (1927)) decision explained that discharging a debt merely transforms the debt. "Discharge" relieves one man of the debt; however, the debt still exists. That burden is transferred to the receiver of the discharge. The people of America were compelled into a system of discharging debts or transferring debt, rather than paying debt. Were they not compelled into deceit and fraud by their very servants, the government of the United States? We will elaborate further below.

Prior to this event, the symbol of the dollar was $. The two vertical lines represented the two Pillars of Hercules. Some believe the two lines could represent the two pillars in Solomon's Temple, representing both form and substance.

Nevertheless, form and substance (gold) on one side balances law on the other side of Solomon's scale. You might remember in your distant past using $ in your writings. (Author RR does). I used to enjoy the cartoons about Scrooge McDuck when I was a kid. I bet you did too!

There are some funny reminders of Uncle Scrooge: http://
www.comicvine.com/uncle-scrooge/29-21543/83490-un-
cle-scrooge/105-75858/

Check out the symbols in the comics! Can't miss that symbol $. And wise old Scrooge didn't hoard paper currency.
Gold filled the bulging bags in his vaults.

In secret, a trick was played on you and me. Look at the
current symbol for the "dollar". It is $ - one vertical line -
representing form only, no substance. What happened?
Did this not follow the government-imposed separation
of precious metal from currency? Might this represent beguiling? Did you ever think of the difference before now?
Do you realize now that the Federal Reserve Bank, with the
involvement of our government, tricked us into using government debt as money?

But the trickery and evil now went nuclear and the people
didn't have a clue. After turning in their gold, their wealth,
their substance, they were given in return a paper commodity. However, this commodity unlike gold, silver, pork
bellies, rice, wheat, etc., did not refer to a substance it represented because it didn't represent anything at all. It's
called a Federal Reserve Note (FRN). In other words, say
a man surrendered a $5 gold coin. He would get back a
piece of paper with "Federal Reserve Note" printed at the
top, and marked "Five dollars". He was forced to use this
piece of paper to "discharge" his debt. He no longer had
gold to actually pay. That wouldn't be so bad if the receiver of the note could go and redeem it for precious metal

coin. So bear with us. Just know that the day before this happened, his house may have been valued at $10,000 worth of gold. The next day, with the acts of his public servants, he can't get substance gold for his home. He gets $10,000 or 10,000 FRNs papers, which do not represent anything of substance. To understand the horror of what just transpired, you need to know what a FRN is….

CHAPTER 13

BANKING AND THE FEDERAL RESERVE ACT

*I sincerely believe, with you, that banking establish-
ments are more dangerous than standing armies. The
monopoly of a single bank is certainly an evil.*
(Thomas Jefferson, 3rd U.S. President)

It's no secret that international bankers were virtually
waging war since the founding of the nation to establish a
central bank. But you're not taught that in school. Popular
president Andrew Jackson almost permanently destroyed
the banker's hopes. But, they were patient and went into
hiding in the shadows. In 1913, after the passage of 70 years,
they were able to get the Congress to pass the Federal Reserve Act. (H.R. 7837 Public, No. 43 December 23, 1913). It
was hustled through during the height of the Christmas
season when many members of Congress had already left,
including the most vocal opposition. Newly elected President Woodrow Wilson was strongly financed by the bankers. He signed the bill.

The story of the bankers and Federal Reserve is just too
dark for this book. You can find an excellent treatise in the
book: The Creature from Jeckyll Island and Secrets of the
Federal Reserve. But the impact of the act is of paramount
importance.

First, the name "Federal" and "Reserve" tricks you into believing that the bank is federal and is keeping something in reserve to back the currency. In fact, the bank is a private corporation. It is essentially a private cartel of mostly foreign bankers with the federal government as a quasi-partner, which passes laws to protect the bankers. It is not an agency of the government. It was an absolutely ingenious strategy by a group of bankers to use that name, and to have the president appoint the board of governors. The latter gives the illusion that the entity is a government agency. Most readers may not believe that the FRB is privately owned. If you find this just too hard to believe we'll let the 9th Circuit Court of Appeals drive it home.

> *"Federal Reserve Banks are not federal instrumentalities for purposes of a Federal Tort Claims Act, but are independent, privately owned and locally controlled corporations in light of fact that direct supervision and control of each bank is exercised by board of directors, federal reserve banks, though heavily regulated, are locally controlled by their member banks, banks are listed neither as "wholly owned" government corporations nor as "mixed ownership" corporations; federal reserve banks receive no appropriated funds from Congress and the banks are empowered to sue and be sued in their own names...." Lewis v. United States, 680 F.2d 1239 (1982)*

Here, a high court tells us that the Federal Reserve Banks are privately owned. And, unlike government agencies, they receive no Congressional funds! It is of paramount importance to accept this as fact when understanding the relationship between the Federal Reserve Bank and the U.S. Government. THE FEDERAL RESERVE BANK IS NOT A PART OF THE U.S. GOVERNMENT.

Next, the issue of control. True there is a Federal Reserve Board appointed by the President. That does not change the ownership! General Motors, a public corporation, could also have an agreement to allow control to someone the President appoints. That would not make it a Federal agency. Furthermore, it still could be a puppet board, for appearances only. Remember the quote of the infamous banker Rothschild on the cover of this book regarding "puppet".

Next, the issue of ownership and situs (the physical place of incorporation). It is public knowledge that the Federal Reserve Bank was set up by a consortium of several international banking families. We know that it is a corporation, and it's private. We don't know where it is incorporated (situs). We can only deduce by the evidence. If the bank were to tell us, there would be no trickery.

Corporations, though they are by statue deemed "persons," are, in fact fictions. That is, they are not flesh and blood. Our existence is said to come straight from the Creator. Corporations are artificial "persons" created by charter and granted their license to exist by government. In that light, there are two types of corporations, domestic and non-domestic. A domestic corporation is created by privilege from a state of the United States or the central government. A non-domestic corporation is created in an offshore jurisdiction.

A domestic corporation exists by a grant (license) from one of the 50 states or District of Columbia. For that privilege, it must pay homage to the state or District. It would be subject to taxes, audits, and all U.S. or state laws that affect corporations. A non-domestic corporation would be subject to the laws of the sovereign that incorporated it. British Petroleum, if incorporated in Great Britain would be subject to the laws of Great Britain. By nature, it would be free to contract with or enter into agreements with any other entity, such as the government of the United States.

As mentioned we don't know where the Federal Reserve Bank/System is incorporated. But we have evidence that it pays no taxes:

Exemption from taxation

Federal Reserve banks, including the capital stock and surplus therein and the income derived therefrom, shall be exempt from Federal, State, and local taxation, except taxes upon real estate. Title 12 section 531 (H.R. 7837 Public, No. 43 December 23, 1913)

So, now you know for sure that the Federal Reserve Bank pays no income taxes, both Federal and State. Note, there is a Federal Reserve Bank in San Francisco. Neither the "Federal Reserve System", nor the "Federal Reserve Bank" is listed in the California Secretary of State's office as doing business in California. It is not listed as a corporation in any state where there is a branch, including Texas where there is a branch in Dallas. Nor is it listed in corporations registered in Washington DC. Yet we know that branches exist in several states. There can only be possibly one of two conclusions as to why the FRB does not pay taxes:

> *1. That the FRB is an exempt foreign corporation.*
> *2. Or, from the Texas Corporation Code Chapter 9 Sub-chapter F section 9.251. It states that "transacting business in interstate commerce" does not constitute transacting business in Texas.*

Hence, no requirement to register or to pay taxes.

The FRB pays no taxes, and is not incorporated in any of the 50 states or the District of Columbia. So, either the FRB is foreign and exempt, or its business (issuing Federal Reserve Notes) is solely one of interstate commerce.

Now we turn to evidence from the great gold grab of 1933.

In 1933, gold was confiscated from all U.S. "Persons." Remember, that the term "Persons" includes corporations. General Motors would have had to turn over its gold. The Federal Reserve did not. In fact, it actually received gold. If GM had to turn in its gold, and the FRB did not, then the move was unconstitutional violating the equal protection clause of the Federal Constitution. This clause would not allow a specific person, such as the FRB, to receive special privileges and immunities over the rest of the citizens of the United States. Of course the gold grab was unconstitutional for other reasons. It was out and out theft. That the FRB received gold is simply icing on the cake that the Bank is not a U.S Person, and would not be subject to, and as one violating the equal protection clause.

Finally, Federal law provides that the banking associations (member banks in the Federal Reserve System) shall buy stock in the Federal Reserve. But note, the purchase must be made in gold or gold certificates. No one else (US citizens and other persons) was legally allowed to possess or transact in gold or gold certificates, or redeem the certificates. Only foreigners! But the FRB was mandated in law to issue stock only upon receipt of gold or gold certificates. (12 USC Section 282).

This provides more evidence as to the nature of the bank. You see, in 1933, not only gold coin was confiscated. Gold certificates became irredeemable for John Q. Public. One day, you could go to the Treasury and get a gold coin for your certificate. The next day, you could not. In fact, the public was ordered to surrender their gold and gold certificates at local banks. Yet, the above-mentioned statute (12 USC Section 282) authorized the FRB to accept gold certificates. That law is still on the books to this day.

What logically follows? Follow closely. Your gold certificates became worthless to you. You were ordered to turn them over to the banks. The banks were enabled to use them to buy stock in the Federal Reserve. It follows clearly that the

U.S. would redeem the gold certificates for the FRB; however, you were forced to surrender them because you were told they were worthless. It should now be apparent that the FRB ended up with the gold, which was surrendered by the American people!

Is it possible that the Depression was a planned nightmare by the bankers? A nightmare to incite the government to force Americans to surrender their wealth? And then their surrendered wealth provided gold and gold certificates to local banks to finance their purchase of FRB stock yet further enriching the international bankers? (Could there be similarities with the current crisis? It has been openly admitted that the government and bankers pushed granting mortgages to unworthy borrowers in the sub-prime mortgage calamity. Now this same government and bankers, which brought you the plague, are openly pushing their cure: dumping all the banking abuse mortgage debt onto the backs of the taxpayers. Do we see the FRB risking *anything* in the current crisis? Even if it didn't get paid back the debt notes it created out of thin air, has it lost anything of value? <u>**We**</u> sure have. **We** have lost something of **major** value – our <u>labor</u> – which is our substance.)

Afterwards, citizens were forced to transact in paper called "Federal Reserve Notes," also known as "legal tender." Yet Congress provided that the FRB receive substance, real gold, rather than the bank's own funny paper (Federal Reserve Notes). Why? Now, we need to examine the Federal Reserve Note.

The Federal Reserve Bank has a product. That product is called a Federal Reserve Note (FRN). This term "product" is important. We turn to definitions in major law dictionaries as well as publications of the FRB itself.

Most Americans think of FRNs as "money" issued by the national government. But are they "money"?

FRNs are defined in U.S. law at Title 12 Section 411 as "obligations of the United States". Let's ask Bouvier's (Law Dictionary) for its definition of obligation:

OBLIGATION. *In its general and most extensive sense, obligation is synonymous with duty. In a more technical meaning, it is a tie which binds us to pay or to do something agreeably to the laws and customs of the country in which the obligation is made.*

If we have an obligation, we are bound to pay. So, can an obligation be money? When looking at a Federal Reserve Note, it has the word dollar on it, doesn't it? Isn't this confusing in the light that it is an obligation as defined in Bouvier's Law Dictionary?

The code further specifies that these obligations shall be *"**denominated**"* in dollars. Denominate is defined as "To issue or express in terms of a given monetary unit." Hence, these notes are expressed as dollars. Well, we're sure that you've seen actors playing a convincing role, sometimes quite convincingly so, in impersonating another. Have you been beguiled into believing that the FRN is really a dollar?

If so, revisit the Coinage Act of 1792. This Act has not been repealed [See Appendix F]. We suggest that you read the Coinage Act to get a sense of the real money of accounts of the United States. There you will find the only definition of a lawful dollar anywhere in U.S. law. ***A dollar is a specific weight of gold or silver.*** End of story.

US Constitution, Article 1, section 8, clause 5
For the United States of America, MONEY is only a Gold or Silver COIN based on the weight/measure standard authorized.

Hence, the FRN is not a dollar, but is denominated as a dollar, or is a **pretend** dollar. It is an illusion of a dollar. This we know to be absolutely true.

But wait! You retort that the notes are printed in the U.S. Treasury. They must be "dollars". The public is steadfastly informed of this fact. That would make one think that the notes are really issued by the government. Hold on!

The FRB actually pays the government to print the notes!

> *"Federal Reserve Banks obtain the notes from our <u>Bureau of Engraving and Printing</u> (BEP). It pays the BEP for the cost of producing the notes…"* (http://www.ustreas. gov/education/faq/currency/legal-tender.shtml)

If you pay a printer, no matter whom, to print your dissertation, who owns it? The print shop or you? Here, the Treasury is acting as the print shop for the FRB. Furthermore, it makes senses that the print shop would be the government. The government has to execute the obligation with a signature! Note the U.S. officials' signature on the obligation. You are surely entitled to print a note and take it to a creditor for consideration. Here, the United States prints the note, which obligates it. Its officers (Treasurer and Secretary of the Treasury) sign it. That binds the United States to the obligation. What a ruse to confuse or hide the truth. Again, if the FRB were an agency of the federal government, it would be receiving its funding from the government to print the "money". The FRB wouldn't directly be paying for it.

The printed pieces of paper are paid for by the FRB, hence, they must be the **property** or __product__ of the FRB. This term product is important as you will subsequently see. Let's have the FRB itself declare its product. http://www.federalreserve.gov/pubs/ifdp/2005/827/ifdp827.pdf page 26

> *"The U.S. economy is the largest economy in the world, with the greatest potential to affect the growth of its trading partners; it is generally less open than the other economies in the sample; we* (Federal Reserve Bank) issue (produce) ***the world's most prominent reserve currency…"*** (notes and emphasis added)

Each note carries a serial number. Let's see how Wikipedia (http://en.wikipedia.org/wiki/Serial_number) defines "serial number":

> *"Serial numbers are valuable in quality control, as once a defect is found in the production of a particular*

> batch of **product,** *the serial number will quickly identify which units are affected. Serial numbers are also used as a deterrent against theft and counterfeit products in that serial numbers can be recorded, and stolen or otherwise irregular goods can be identified."*

There is no serial number to be found on any lawful gold or silver coin. To summarize: The FRB is a private foreign corporation. It took all of the gold of Americans and other persons in 1933, and not one US Citizen, inclusive of any and all domestic corporations, etc., was allowed to own gold. Checking the websites for the Secretaries of State, one will not find any of the Federal Reserve Banks registered as a business or corporation within any of the states. Thus, it is impossible to find a registered agent to serve in the event one has been damaged by the FRB and wants to sue-out the claim. This is compelling evidence that it is a foreign corporation, in that it is not registered with the state to do business. That is unlike every other form of domestic business, which must be registered with the individual state's Secretary of State. We know that there is an exclusion for business filings for entities dealing in interstate commerce. Hence, the activities of the bank (FRNs) must be empowered by the commerce clause of the Constitution. The FRB issues the world's most prominent reserve currency. The FRB pays the US government print shop to print those FRNs. It marks each with a serial number. Serial numbers deal with products. Conclusion: Federal Reserve Notes are products of the foreign Federal Reserve Bank used to transact interstate and foreign commerce.

So now we have evidence in law that these notes are private property of the FRB. Now what is a note? Blacks Law dictionary (3rd) tells us that a note as used here means a promissory note. What does Bouvier's Law Dictionary say about the latter?

> **PROMISSORY NOTE**, *contracts. A written promise to pay a certain sum of money, at a future time, unconditionally. It is dated and signed by the maker. He who makes the promise is called the maker, and he to whom it is made is the payee.*

So we now see that the FRN is a contract, a written promise to pay a certain sum of money. A common term for this is an IOU.

In all financial documents, the lender, which is the creditor, is at the top. The maker, the debtor is second. Look at the FRN in your possession. Who is the creditor at the top? The bank! The debtor is the United States of America. Look again at the image of the FRN. And see who the creditor is, and who the debtor is.

This obligation is signed (executed) by 2 officers of the United States, as any debt note is signed. We included the back of the FRN to point out the words "IN GOD WE TRUST." Whose God? All things in the universe have both form and substance. If God Almighty requires both form and substance in our transactions, then who or what is in power over form (FRNs) only? A picture of you is of your 'form' (illusion), and no one would mistake that the picture was actually you; however, the flesh and blood you is 'form and substance,' it is the actual you.

Conclusion from the preceding few paragraphs? The FRN is actual property belonging to the FRB. It is evidence of the obligation of the United States of America to the bank. It is a note of debt. It must be ultimately returned to the bank to satisfy the obligation of the USA unless the bank is keeping it in circulation to gather perpetual interest.

This is so ghoulish that you might not believe the authors, so we'll present confirmation in excerpts from Congressman

Louis McFadden as recorded in the Congressional Record:

> *"Mr. Chairman, when you hold a $10 Federal Reserve note in your hand you are holding a piece of paper which sooner or later is going to cost the United States Government $10 in gold....*
>
> *The sack of the United States by the Federal Reserve Board and the Federal Reserve banks is the greatest crime in history.*
>
> *Mr. Chairman, a serious situation confronts the House of Representatives today. We are trustees of the people and the rights of the people are being taken away from them. Through the Federal Reserve Board and the Federal Reserve banks, the people are losing the rights guaranteed to them by the Constitution. Their property has been taken from them without due process of law. Mr. Chairman, common decency requires us to examine the public accounts of the Government and see what crimes against the public welfare have and are being committed.*
>
> *Mr. Chairman, when a Chinese merchant sells human hair to a Paris wigmaker and bills him in dollars, the Federal Reserve banks can buy his bill against the wigmaker and then use that bill as collateral for the Federal Reserve notes. The United States Government thus pays the Chinese merchant the debt of the*

wigmaker and gets nothing in return except a shady title to the Chinese hair.

Mr. Chairman, if a German brewer ships beer to this country or anywhere else in the world and draws his bill for it in dollars, the Federal Reserve banks will buy that bill and use it as collateral for Federal Reserve notes. Thus, they compel our Government to pay the German brewer for his beer.

On April 27, 1932, the Federal Reserve outfit sent $750,000, belonging to American bank depositors, in gold to Germany. A week later, another $300,000 in gold was shipped to Germany in the same way. About the middle of May $12,000,000 in gold was shipped to Germany by the Federal Reserve Board and the Federal Reserve banks. Almost every week there is a shipment of gold to Germany. These shipments are not made for profit on the exchange since the German marks are below parity with the dollar. The Federal Reserve Board and the Federal Reserve banks lately conducted an anti-hoarding campaign here. Then they took that extra money which they had persuaded the American people to put into the banks and they sent it to Europe along with the rest. In the last several months, they have sent $1,300,000,000 in gold to their foreign employers, their foreign masters, and every dollar of that gold belonged to the people of the United States and was unlawfully taken from them." **McFadden 6-10-1932**

http://www.modernhistoryproject.org/mhp/Article
Display.php?Article=McFadden1932

From the above, it is clear that the Federal Reserve Bank
would buy the bill of foreign merchants with FRNs. The
security for those FRNs was the questionable bill, or the
products that the bill liened. The US government had to
redeem the Federal Reserve Notes in gold. Tons of (the
citizen's) gold was thereby shipped overseas. Our government traded our gold for liens on title to foreign, often
consumable, products. How could anyone go overseas
to claim hypothecated property? Our gold vanished. The
government and bank did not pursue collection or seizure for the hypothecated liened overseas transaction. (It
might prove difficult to go after the hair in a wig!) However, government sure comes after us, now the chattel
property.

The Hon. E.J. Hill, a former Member of the House,
confirmed:

> *"They are obligations of the Government for which the
> United States has received nothing and for the pay-
> ment of which at any time it assumes the responsibil-
> ity looking to the Federal Reserve to recoup itself."*

Finally, we go back just a few years from McFadden in the
early 1930's for events that are sure to make your blood
boil. The following is from a book entitled A Bubble that
Broke the World – By: Garet Garrett

OPERATING THE GOLDEN GOOSE – Page 99
(POST MORATORIUM)

"The Federal Reserve System has been threatened with raids upon its gold supply by foreign nations, notable by France. There has been that threatening situation, the conjecture–and it is a conjecture–being that that country wanted to affect our situation with respect to reparations and with respect to her indebtedness to the United States. I do not make the assertion. I say that it is conjecture. The officials of the Bank of France have simply outwitted the officials of the Federal Reserve System of this country." SENATOR CARTER GLASS, Formerly Secretary of the Treasury, moving in the United States Senate, February 17, 1932, the Glass-Steagal bill, an emergency act to protect the American gold reserve.

To the further education of American credit abroad enter these autumnal sights and experience, videlicet:

2. The rationally impossible spectacle of debtor nations raiding the gold reserves of a creditor nation while the creditor is self-bound and helpless under an agreement not to collect its debts from them.*

[* Notes from the authors: In the early 1930's the USA created Gold Certificates out of thin air, and lent the same to France. Under the terms of the loan, there was a year moratorium in which France did not have to pay the loan back.

What France, the debtor nation, then did was to return to the USA with the Gold certificates. It then redeemed all of the certificates pulling ships loaded with the Gold of the People of the United States out of the Banks of the United States. This single act caused the nation to suspend the Gold Standard.]

We would like to quote more on this; however, the copyright laws protect the intellectual rights of the owner.

Let's repeat the above limited information for clarity. France gets a loan in gold certificates. France is supposed to begin payback a year later. During that year, though, it presents the certificates for redemption. The gold coffers of the United States were depleted. We don't have enough gold to cover the certificates of our own people. Our own people get wiped out with certificates that they can't redeem. What happened to all that gold? We don't have the answer. However, it should be obvious to you that something terribly more than malevolent was at foot with the gold reserves of the greatest creditor nation (America) in the world at that time. WHERE IS ALL THAT GOLD NOW?

Finally, we now provide, direct from the Constitution, all the enumerated powers of Congress:

> *"The Congress shall have Power To lay and collect Taxes, Duties, Imposts and Excises, to pay the Debts and provide for the common Defence and general Welfare of the United States; but all Duties, Imposts*

and Excises shall be uniform throughout the United States;"

⁻ To borrow money on the credit of the United States;

⁻ To regulate Commerce with foreign Nations, and among the several States, and with the Indian Tribes;

⁻ To establish an uniform Rule of Naturalization, and uniform Laws on the subject of Bankruptcies throughout the United States;

⁻To coin Money, regulate the Value thereof, and of foreign Coin, and fix the Standard of Weights and Measures;

⁻ To provide for the Punishment of counterfeiting the Securities and current Coin of the United States;

⁻ To establish Post Offices and Post Roads;

⁻ To promote the Progress of Science and useful Arts, by securing for limited Times to Authors and Inventors the exclusive Right to their respective Writings and Discoveries;

⁻ To constitute Tribunals inferior to the supreme Court;

— To define and punish Piracies and Felonies committed on the high Seas, and Offenses against the Law of Nations;

— To declare War, grant Letters of Marque and Reprisal, and make Rules concerning Captures on Land and Water;

— To raise and support Armies, but no Appropriation of Money to that Use shall be for a longer Term than two Years;

— To provide and maintain a Navy;

— To make Rules for the Government and Regulation of the land and naval Forces;

—To provide for calling forth the Militia to execute the Laws of the Union, suppress Insurrections and repel Invasions;

— To provide for organizing, arming, and disciplining the Militia, and for governing such Part of them as may be employed in the Service of the United States, reserving to the States respectively, the Appointment of the Officers, and the Authority of training the Militia according to the discipline prescribed by Congress;

— To exercise exclusive Legislation in all Cases whatsoever, over such District (not exceeding ten Miles square) as may, by Cession of particular States, and *the acceptance of Congress, become the Seat of the Government of the United States, and to exercise like Authority over all Places purchased by the Consent of the Legislature of the State in which the Same shall be, for the Erection of Forts, Magazines, Arsenals, dock-Yards, and other needful Buildings; And*

¬ To make all Laws which shall be necessary and proper for carrying into Execution the foregoing Powers, and all other Powers vested by this Constitution in the Government of the United States, or in any Department or Officer thereof.

Please see also: www.usconstitution.net/const.html

Clearly the powers delegated dealt almost exclusively with uniform standards of weights and measures, defense and commerce. Congress had the power to borrow money. Now, we ask you the following: **Where in these enumerated powers is there any authority to lend money?** THERE IS NONE! Would "treason" be an applicable term for lending money without authority? Do you see any authority for the Congress to confiscate your property? And where is there authority to do the 99.9% of other shenanigans that the Congress does? We don't see it (other than commerce as we will explain). If you do, please email us on the website.

Chapter 14

*"Those who surrender freedom for security
will surely have neither."*
(Benjamin Franklin, perhaps the most famous of the
Founding Fathers)

When you go to purchase something with FRNs, you are actually using an IOU of the government to obtain possession of your purchase. Now you know that we have been tricked into using government debt as money! Have you been honorable in your purchase? Did you actually pay for the item by giving the seller someone else's IOU? If you have taken something for yourself, yet tendered someone else's IOU, how would that fit into the common law regarding theft? Obviously, theft is done with knowledge. Clearly in these matters you didn't know, until now, that you were part of a scheme devised by unseen hands to lift the labor of others. Furthermore, the theft is not to your benefit, but to an unseen creditor. You are being used by trickery. But now you know. And it is important to consider how to fix the wrong, which we will address in the chapter on "Redemption and Remedy".

Now remember that FRNs are IOUs from the government to the FRB. The Congress compelled all Americans to use someone else's IOU to "pay" (discharge) debt, placing all

Americans into debt forever. The seller NEVER gets paid. He only receives an IOU, a debt of the United States payable to the FRB. It should now be perfectly clear. The government went belly up to the FRB in 1933. As part of the "reorganization" the FRB allowed the government to continue operations with the bank's private script. This printed script is loaned to its debtor at interest, creating a condition of perpetual bondage of the government. Worse, rather than reveal the truth to the people, the government roped the people into the same ghastly scheme. The government could have, and should have been forthcoming with the horrific skullduggery it committed with the People's gold. It did not. The government blamed the people for "hoarding" gold rather than reveal it shipped out the gold it held in trust. It concealed the truth from the People. By confiscating (stealing) the gold (wealth) from the people, the government destroyed the American people's ability to pay debt, since there is no substance backing the notes. The American people instantly became debtors. The only backing of FRNs is your willingness to accept them. This truth is actually published in Federal Reserve publications, referenced in this book. (Modern Money Mechanics –http://www.truthsetsusfree.com/ModernMoneyMechanics.pdf). That means the notes are backed by your labor. And if you don't want these notes, you are forced to accept them anyway. Hence, the term, "fiat currency". Wikipedia:

> *"The terms **fiat currency** and **fiat money** relate to types of currency or money whose usefulness results, not from any intrinsic value or guarantee that it can be converted into gold or another currency, but in-*

*stead from a government's order (fiat) that it must be
accepted as a means of payment."*

Do we call this beguiling, trickery, illusion? It is not a matter of willingness to accept these debt notes either. You
are compelled by government fiat (force) to accept something admitted as worthless for your labor.

Remember this - before all Americans turned their gold
certificates in, the individual Americans were the creditors.
The banks and the Treasury were the debtors to us. They
only held our gold on deposit in trust for us. When we
were **_compelled_** to turn our gold certificates in, the banks
instantly became the creditors and we became the debtors. It all happened in the twinkling of an eye. We, the authors, are astounded that the American people didn't react
with loud voices.

Oh, but it gets much worse than that. For starters, these
debt notes are issued by the FRB at interest. Do you remember the example we gave about a man borrowing
a hoe and having to pay interest by returning two hoes?
Where does the other hoe come from? Does the first one
reproduce? Do you remember example 2 in the prologue.
If not, go back and read it now. **This is a brand new animal: the FRB *charging interest* on debt it creates out of
thin air while having nothing at risk.**

In the case of the FRB, pretend for a moment that its loan is
actually real money to society. It loans out 1 million dollars
at 3% interest. If only 1,000,000.00 bills were printed, and

no other bills exist, how does one pay back the $ 30,000.00 in interest, or the entire sum of $ 1,030,000.00 at the end of the year? It can't. NO ONE CAN! The only way that $ 30,000 in interest can appear is if new "money" is issued. That means more "money" has to be printed and borrowed by society to pay the previous years interest - that $ 30,000.00 unprinted bills that did not exist in the economy. Can you now see the evil in usury? Can you see why it was forbidden? Can you see why it can be used to destroy? Can you see that the government is locked into a PERMANENT state of bankruptcy reorganization because of perpetual insolvency? Would a bankruptcy judge ever let you perpetually reorganize?

And in the case of FRNs, you are beguiled into thinking that you are actually receiving a loan of money. You are, in truth, receiving a loan of IOUs. You are getting debt notes of the USA or more aptly put credit notes due the FRB. And what really are these notes? They are contracts, commercial instruments, very similar to a bill of exchange, created out of thin air. The FRB creates an imaginary debt out of thin air, gets back interest that can never be completely paid. We've shown you that the FRB will only take gold for its stock (ownership interest in the corporation). Additionally, the bank would only take the interest on its notes in gold! And that's been true since 1933. The FRB won't take its own notes of trickery as interest. It takes your substance. It won't take its notes of trickery from banking associations for stock. It only takes gold. The FRB demands SOMETHING for NOTHING!

Now, can you sit there and still say in the light of the gold confiscation of US entities, which included men and fictions, that the FRB is a U.S. entity? Clearly, the FRB is the creditor of the USA. So, is the FRB superior and foreign to the United States? The evidence should be crystal clear to you now that the veil of trickery has been lifted. As creditor, it is foreign, as creditor it is the master. The FRB did not have to turn over its gold to the USA. The reverse was true; it received gold from the USA and its people.

A creditor cannot be subject to the rules and regulations of the debtor. It doesn't work that way. The FRB clearly is an entity foreign to the USA. The USA has become hopelessly indebted to the creditor. Now we will prove that you have been beguiled into the same insolvent status as the bankrupt USA. We now reveal greed, beguiling, deceit, trickery, and malevolence of galactic proportions.

CHAPTER 15

JURISDICTIONAL RAMIFICATIONS OF USING FRNs

*If the American People ever allow private banks to control the issue of their money, first by inflation and then by deflation, the banks and corporations that will grow up around (the banks), will deprive the people of their property until their children will wake up homeless on the continent their fathers conquered … I believe that banking institutions are **more dangerous** to our liberties than standing armies. Already they have raised up a moneyed aristocracy that has set the government in defiance.* (Thomas Jefferson, 3rd U.S. President)

Remember, once upon a time we were within the common law of the land. Admiralty law was/is the law of the seas in a time of war or emergency. Now we point out a few major court cases.

"In this country revenue causes has so long been the subject of Admiralty cognizance, that congress considered them as CIVIL CAUSES OF ADMIRALTY AND MARITIME JURISDICTION, The Huntress, 12 Fed. Case 984 @ 992 & 989, (Case No. 6,914)(D.Me. 1840): This explicitly tells us that government revenue operations arise out of Admiralty and Admiralty alone!

Modern Supreme Court cases tell us that Internal Revenue forfeiture actions commence in Admiralty. After jurisdiction (admiralty) is obtained, the case "takes on the "**character**" of a "civil" action." Is the term "character" not synonymous with the taking on of a disguise? Don't actors take on characters in their movies by disguise? Did you previously know that the IRS falls within Admiralty? How could you if you were tricked by "the character of" a "civil" action. Once Admiralty, always admiralty. Jurisdiction obtained under one system of law (Admiralty) can never be transferred. If the case is to be under another system, it must commence as a new case under that new system. What is happening here is that they have made it look like one thing (civil) while they move against their target doing another (Admiralty). A wolf in sheep's clothing is still a wolf.

You likely know people who have lost homes and property to the IRS. Did you ever hear mentioned the word "Admiralty"? Did they ever even know? You know that you are subject to the Internal Revenue Service. How did that happen if the IRS operates in Admiralty? Where is your international commercial contract?

This perplexing question was solved by RM who followed the hints leaked by the Supreme Court in United States of America, Libelant v $3976.62 In Currency, One 1960 Ford Station Wagon, 37 F.R.D. 564. A car and currency were seized on the land. The court stated the authorization to seize came from "Admiralty rules in the Federal Rules of Civil Procedure." Specifically the trail leads to "Supplemental Rules for Certain Admiralty and Maritime Claims." It specifically led to "Notes to Rule C". It states that suits may be brought to enforce any maritime lien. And the trail dead ends in a deep, dark, almost impossible to find hole in paragraph "e": "***Suits founded on mere maritime hypothecation.***" (http://www.law.cornell.edu/rules/frcp/ACRuleC.htm)

Remember, maritime is the same as Admiralty. The latter is what the jurisdiction is called in a time of emergency. Roosevelt declared an emergency in 1933. It has NEVER been lifted (Senate Report 93-549) (U.S. Government Printing Office, November 19.1973 24-509 O). Admiralty is a military designation for the maritime jurisdiction that is enforced during time of emergency. Such times involve a military (or force-controlled) state of affairs. The "Admiral" obviously is military.

Now, who would ever think that IRS actions are Admiralty? That sure seems wild. If so, how did you get into Admiralty? We must connect the dots to that obscure paragraph "**e**".

The IRS claimed property based on "mere maritime hypothecation". When Ron uncovered this link, he called me (RR) at 5am to declare the discovery. I jumped out of bed. I never had heard the term before. However, I intuitively knew exactly what it meant. We both laughed so hard we got dizzy.

Go back to Chapters 3 and 6 where we first described hypothecation. It means property in international commerce that is liened since it was never paid for. The lien would follow it forever until it was paid. The creditor could come and seize his unpaid goods at any time. The mortgage on your home is a private hypothecation. The house is liened until paid for.

So how do you get into this situation? Two ways. First, you owe a tax. Second, what you think is your property is not yours. Remember, the currency, Federal Reserve Notes. They are the property of the creditor. They are the obligations due him! They are liened to him! They might be in your possession but you don't have title, rights and interest in his property! The creditor is merely collecting back what is his and liened by hidden hypothecation. You are transacting in property (Federal Reserve Notes) that don't belong to you!!!

What about the car that was taken in Admiralty? It too was hypothecated. The "buyer" "purchased" it with the obligations of the United States (FRNs) owed to the creditor (FRB). The "buyer" (you) never paid for the (your) car. You used another entity's (United States) IOU (FRNs) to get it. There is a lien attached to the car by the use of the IOU. The IOU was never paid to the creditor. And, somehow you violated the terms of the privilege of using the IOU as well as the liened property (car). Perhaps you did not pay your income taxes or any fee/fine for anything the government requires, or failed to obtain a permit. The lien attaches like glue, or more aptly described, like "$lime" to whatever property it touched. The creditor then moves on the lien and claims his secured property.

In the common law, had you paid in gold, all of the intrinsic qualities of your sovereign unliened gold would transfer into the car. Your gold coin granted you the title, rights and interests in the coin, and those qualities transferred to your car. Thus, you would own possession and all title, rights, and interests in your car. No liens transferred in the transaction. The debt would be extinguished. When you "discharged" the debt with FRNs, its intrinsic qualities, too, would transfer into the thing acquired.   Since the FRN has a hidden lien, which is intrinsic in all of the Federal Reserve Notes, that intrinsic quality transfers into the very thing you are buying. Now isn't that the ultimate beguiling? You are unaware of this fact. However, it is a fact that the property you have just "bought" and presently believe you own is liened to the Creditor.

The intrinsic properties of the FRN transfers into the thing acquired, or transacted for. The FRN is a liened instrument. You traded the property of the FRB for the car. If I lend you a hoe and you trade it for someone else's rake, I can't get the hoe back, but that rake you "paid" for with my hoe surely is mine! It's clear that the car becomes the security for that FRB property you passed off. This is trickery and deceit of the highest order.

CHAPTER 16

ADHESIVE CONTRACTS ($LIME STICKING TO YOU)

"You are a <u>den of vipers</u>. I intend to rout you out and by the Eternal God I will rout you out. If the people only understood the rank injustice of our money and banking system, there would be a revolution before morning."
(Andrew Jackson, 7th U.S. President)

The phrase 'adhesive contract' may be a mystery to you. Most people think their duties in a contract are the terms and conditions they sign the contract under. That's true in the common law, but it's not true in commercial law. When you are involved in commerce, you are deemed to know the law.

Take the example of your purchase of a DVD. You own the use of the DVD. Being your "property" you begin to make copies of it and sell them. Is this legal? Of course not. You are subject to the crime of copyright infringement. The rights to the DVD belong to the copyright holder. The DVD is his intellectual property. You cannot plead ignorance of the law, even if you truly didn't know. The court will tell you that ignorance of the law is no excuse. There was an implied or adhesive contract that came with your purchase. You violated that contract by making copies. You are guilty, plain and simple, whether you knew that implied contract existed or not.

The same is true for one who buys a pirated DVD. He cannot even _possess_ that property without paying the real owner (copyright holder) for the rights to possess it. Is this unconscionable? No. It is commercial law. The buyer had a duty to know or at least note the © on the label for dealing in commerce. The same, obviously, is true for copyrighted books.

When you transact in commerce, you are presumed by the court to know the law. Indeed, you have a duty to know the law. You are bound by adhesive commercial contracts and duties that may, in fact, be **deliberately** hidden from you.

Chapter 17

"Paper is poverty,…it is only the ghost of money and not money itself."
"Experience has proved to us that a dollar of silver disappears for every dollar of paper emitted."
(Thomas Jefferson, 3rd U.S. President)

The Congressional Research Service (CRS) updated a report on May 7, 2001, by legislative attorney John Lucky. (http://www.givemeliberty.org/NoRedress/HistoricalDocs/AAA--CRS-FAQ-Rebuttal.pdf). It's called "Frequently asked Questions about the Federal Income Tax." We present one section only, which we have discussed earlier. This is to drive it home. Then we pose questions that were not addressed (deliberately?) in the report.

3. What does the court mean when it states that the income tax is in the nature of an excise tax?

"An excise tax is a tax levied on the manufacture, sale, or consumption of a commodity or any various taxes on privileges often assessed in the form of a license or fee. In other words, it is a tax on doing something to property or on the privilege of holding some property or doing some act, not a tax on the property itself. The tax is not on the property directly, but rather it is a tax on the transaction.

When a court refers to an income tax as being in the nature of an excise, it is merely stating that the tax is not on the property itself."

Now turn to a U.S. Supreme Court case (Flint v. Stone Tracy Co., 220 US 107 (1911))

"Excises are taxes laid upon the manufacture, sale or consumption of commodities within the country, upon licenses to pursue certain occupations, and upon corporate privileges;"

The CRS summarized court decisions. It tells us that the income tax is in the nature of an excise tax. You see above the definition of excise. We offer this question for which we have not the answer. "If men and women are engaging in commerce, could that be a privilege?"

The FRN is a foreign-owned commodity in international commerce. It is outright owned by a private corporation. We have seen compelling evidence that said corporation is foreign to the United States. Could the activities of the purchase and/or sale of this commodity with your labor be the subject of excise? Could the consumption/transfer of this commodity, and/or their transfer in inheritance or gifts be the activities subject to excise? Does the nature of the FRN fit the term "commodity" subject to excise in Flint V. Stone Tracy? Is it possible that we may be buying these FRNs when we are exchanging our labor for them at the end of the work week, and alternately, selling these FRNs for our food, shelter, pleasure, etc.? Would the use of this commodity be deemed a taxable event under excise tax?

Pretend this property (FRNs) were truly yours after you had paid a tax upon receiving it. Why then would that property be subject to another tax upon you leaving a large sum of "what is yours" to your children as an inheritance? In other words, is transacting (transferring) in or with this foreign owned property (FRNs) a commercial activity subjecting you to commercial regulatory (tax and other) laws of the United States? Is use of the FRB's property (FRNs), which is in international commerce, the act that places you "subject to the jurisdiction thereof?" Would that render you a citizen of a corporation (United States) subject to all its rules and regulations? Would you be considered in contract with that corporation and subject to Admiralty/Maritime law? Would this then eliminate any claim you have to your own labor? Would this also eliminate your ties to the law of the land and its solemn Rights?

Consider an answer to one of the most perplexing questions regarding taxes ever. Americans have been bewildered for generations how they can be taxed for bartering, no currency involved. After all, it is an "even" exchange, say a car for a home remodel. So if no gain or profit, how is that transaction legally taxed? Oops, no one knew that the car was liened, as were all the products for remodel. And those bartering didn't know that they were insolvent, in debt to a hidden creditor, and could only contract subject to the creditor's terms and conditions. Could the income tax on barter be a transfer tax on the property that is liened for (property of) the Creditor? A tax similar to the transfer of FRNs (property of the FRB) from one to another? Remember, you not owning anything places a hidden third party to all your transactions you conduct with property of the Creditor. Is the Creditor the real party in interest, the lien holder or "legal" owner, who permits your use (possession) and transactions (transfer) by (taxable) privilege, not by Right?

We close this chapter with this easy to understand analogy. You have a mortgage on your house. The real owner is the creditor until the house is paid off. You are allowed to sell it and the next "buyer" can assume the loan for an assumption fee. So, you must inform the creditor and pay him the transfer "fee." Each subsequent "buyer" must pay the assumption fee. Does this also fit the scheme of the "inheritance" or gift tax? Are you paying a transfer fee (excise tax) for the privilege of transferring the creditor's liened property to your new assignee?

Chapter 18

"He who seeks shall Find"

….Jesus

Our purpose has been to lead you to be able to see the invisible, to recognize illusion. When you look in the mirror you know that what you see is an illusion. It looks like you; it has the form of you, but not the _substance_ of you.

As you have seen, the $ (dollars) that were used until 1933 had both form and substance. A subtle change that few would take heed of sometime after 1933 was the substitution of $ for $. The former has form only. A Jell-O mold has form, but without the Jell-O, it lacks substance or the real value. Seeing the mold at a distance, and unable to see that it lacked substance, you could be tricked. Jesus said, "He who seeks shall find." That applies to every aspect of life. What backs the $ of today? If you don't seek, you might not find.

Let's seek the answer in publications of the Federal Reserve itself. Here's a clip and paste quote from <u>Modern Money Mechanics.</u>

> *"In the United States neither paper currency nor deposits have value as commodities. Intrinsically, a dollar bill is just a piece of paper, deposits merely book*

entries. Coins do have some intrinsic value as metal, but generally far less than their face value.

What, then, makes these instruments - checks, paper money, and coins - acceptable at face value in payment of all debts and for other monetary uses? Mainly, it is the confidence people have that they will be able to exchange such money for other financial assets and for real goods and services whenever they choose to do so."

When you seek information directly from the bea$t (the international banking cartel of which the Federal Reserve is key), you discover that the "commodities" of paper currency and demand deposits have <u>no value</u> other than the "confidence" that someone else will accept it in trade. It is up to you to accept it at face value. The bank admits that coins have some value as metal, but "far less" than their face value. Confusing? The bank is telling you that the stamped face value of the coin is a lie! The metal of the coin is worth far less than what numerical value is stamped upon its face.

Here we connect more dots. A dollar by law is a fixed weight of gold or silver (Coinage Act of 1792, Appendix F). The FRB herein openly admits that the value of the base metal of the current coin of the United States is far less than the face value. In real law, the coin would be gold or silver. Is this not illusion and trickery? And paper currency? It's even worse than coin. Today's dollar bill is "just a piece of paper," openly admitted by the creditor. Hence, it only has the value of the paper, not even of the base metal of clad coins. Your checking account consists only of "book entries," no substance. You are "paying" for "real goods and services" with a mere piece of paper or a book entry backed by pieces of paper. It is form only, no substance. Is this not fraud? Are you participating in it?

Let's follow the transition from a physical mark to the invisible mark. We have seen the symbol $, bearing two pillars for the *form* and *substance* of money. Now, lose the pillar for *substance* and we have only the symbol $ (mark) representing the *form* only of money. This symbol, $ is $ubterfuge? Perhaps for bea$t? Remember that a mark brands property. The real mark of the Bea$t will be invisible. Now, connect the following thoughts:

We know that the $ is property of the FRB. The paper, Federal Reserve Note, is marked with the Creditor's/Lender's/Owner's name, Federal Reserve, at the top. When you participate in the fraud of the system, by acquiring "property" with it, you used another person's (actually an entity) property to do so. What you received was not paid for and carries a lien by maritime hypothecation. It doesn't belong to you. What your employer "paid" you does not belong to you! Can you guess now what the invisible mark is? *It's the invisible hypothecated lien!!!!!* It marks your right hand when you receive the $limed bank note! Everything in the USA and, as you will see, in the world, carries this invisible mark. This mark claims what you think you own as property of the FRB. Your employer is unknowingly participating in theft of your labor on behalf of the creditor, as you unwittingly do with others in subsequent transfers of the diseased currency.

A cow branded with the symbol '$' from the $ubterfuge Ranch wanders into your field. Can the $ubterfuge ranch retrieve it? Certainly. It is the $ubterfuge Rancher's property. They can simply march on to your field and collect the cow. Can they allow you to use the cow for its milk? Certainly, but remember you will never own that cow; you only get to use it. Surely, you will have to pay for its use. Using the cow is considered an activity. Hence, the $ubterfuge Ranch can levy a use tax upon the activity. The nature of a thing is its essential qualities or properties. The indirect tax includes many forms of taxation, each of which has the same essential qualities on how these taxes are applied to the thing taxed. "Among 'indirect taxes' are sales, excise, turnover, value added, franchise, stamp, transfer, inventory, or equipment tax, a border tax , etc." (19 Code of Federal Regulations Subpart A—Scope and definitions, Title 19 – Customs Duties)

Indirect taxes are included in the price paid for the goods or services by its final purchaser. Cigarettes and alcohol have stamps on them. That stamp is a tax and is attached to and included in the item before it reaches the market. You, as a consumer will not necessarily know the amount of that tax because it is hidden in the shelf price (when the item is sitting on the shelf). That is a tax that is passed on as an "indirect" tax to the consumer.

As seen in the example below, a "Use" tax (a tax on just using an item, product etc.) is an indirect tax. When one uses a thing like a lawn mower to cut his lawn, the activity would be "the mowing of the lawn." Hopefully you can see that the activity of mowing the lawn is different than the thing involved in the mowing of the lawn, which is the mower. So the "mower" or equipment is different than the "activity", which is the use of the equipment.

So when we say that a "Use" tax is an indirect tax, given the mower example above, that tax is not on the mower, but it is on the activity, the mowing. So concerning the "income tax", where it is stated that it is in the nature of an indirect tax, this means that it is not a tax on the mower, but is a tax on the use of the mower. "Use" tax = indirect tax = activity tax. (Federal courts have affirmatively held that the "income tax" ***is in the nature of an indirect tax***.") We have seen the elaboration on this from the Congressional Research Institute.

If you violate the terms in the use of the thing (FRN) the creditor allows you to use, he can repossess it – in Admiralty! Why is it repossessed in Admiralty? It is repossessed in Admiralty because the contract and commodity both fall under commercial law, the law that deals with contracts across state or national lines. The symbol '$' is a foreign product of the foreign corporation, the Federal Reserve. If you read the reference material we cited in the appendix, it will be clear to you that the majority of the owners of the FRB were foreigners in international banking. However, that's not the reason it is foreign. As a corporation not created by the U.S. or state governments, it IS foreign to the U.S. government.

Every contract transacted with the '$' "money" crosses national lines because the notes come from a foreign jurisdiction. That is precisely what subjects the one using the "$' money to the law of Admiralty. And, Admiralty is the jurisdiction/authority to hear cases in international law. No questions asked; and, without your permission, the cow is taken. That's because your permission is not required when the contract/lien is violated by you, just as your permission is not required in a foreclosure.

Remember, every '$' dollar has an equivalent lien upon it. A $1.00 bill has a one-dollar lien hidden upon it, as a $5.00 bill has a hidden five-dollar lien. This is how the Creditor protects his property. As a result, when you use FRNs to buy food, purchase a car or a house, pay your doctor or dentist, or the hospital when your baby was delivered, you contracted within the commercial jurisdiction/authority. And that is the Admiralty jurisdiction! Further, each time you transact using the $lime, also known as the Federal Reserve Note, you are directly contracting with the party that owns that $lime, the Federal Reserve, which FRN product came from outside the jurisdiction of the United States. Every transaction that you have done or shall do with the $lime and everything you have sold or bought has moved into the Admiralty (international commerce) jurisdiction. But even worse, it moves you personally into the Admiralty jurisdiction, because of the hidden liens that are carried along with every note that you have used. You are the surety (security) for the lien, pledging to make it good. You like a corporate officer can be personally held to answer. ***THE HIDDEN LIEN IS THE INVISIBLE MARK OF THE BEA$T!***

The Mark of the Bea$t renders you the chattel (property) of the Bea$t.

When your child is delivered and you have given your insurance card, or made your check payable to the hospital, the lien attaches to the head of your child as he/she moves out through the birthing canal. He/she now becomes the 'thing' upon which the lien has been placed. (We will have more on this in a subsequent chapter). He/she now belongs to, and is the chattel of the Federal Reserve Bank. That is because the FRB owns the notes, which have the hidden liens, which were used in the transaction at the hospital. There is not one thing that now does not have the hidden lien upon it. All real estate, all personal property, all humans have received the Mark of the Beast. And 'none shall be able to buy or sell' without this mark. It is the ultimate $lime, and the ultimate beguiling, because you cannot perceive this kind of $lime with your senses. You cannot see it, touch it, taste it, feel it, nor smell it, but it is there on everything and every place. They own it all, **including you!**

HERE IS AN EXPLANATION OF THE MARK OF THE BEAST:

U → Contract ← N   You (U) and your neighbor (N) contract. Your neighbor is going to paint your house for $1,500.00

Contract = $1,500.00

The contract is worth $1,500. However, the $1,500.00 worth of notes belongs to the FRB. It is their product and Americans only have the use of this foreign product. The people can never own them. The $1,500.00 is 1,500 IOUs. The FRB has secured their interest over the notes and the 'things' that are sold or bought with hidden liens, which is called hypothecation. This makes the FRB the Creditor and protects its interests. The FRB takes a legal interest (by lien) in what its notes "purchases" since that is its property until the FRB is repaid for its issued "obligation."

FRB/Admiralty

The Federal Reserve Bank is a foreign corporation. When you use its products (FRNs) in any contract, the contract and you attaches to the Creditor, because its interests are protected by liens. Thus, the Creditor/FRB becomes the primary party of interest in the contract. You and your neighbor have an illusion of an inferior interest because you will not actually be paying for anything in this contract. Though the Creditor is not named in the contract, he is the lien holder. Why? Because its products (FRNs) were or will be used for the very 'thing' that you and your neighbor had contracted. It is the status of the parties that determines the jurisdiction. Your status may be a US citizen. The Creditor, which is the FRB, is a corporation foreign to the USA. (This has nothing to do with being owned by non-Americans.) This mix moves the contract outside of the United States into International Law/ Admiralty. You and your neighbor now have a contract, with a hidden agenda. Neither of you can ever pay for the contract. The contract subjects you both to International Law. And, you and he are moved within and under the Admiralty jurisdiction, which shall hear issues that may rise upon the contract. (See the United States Constitution Article III, § 2 Original Jurisdiction, Cases of Admiralty). By using the Federal Reserve Notes you are directly dealing with the Creditor (FRB) even though you do not know this hidden part of the contract. This subjects you and your neighbor both to transacting with a foreign corporation, which is a taxable event.

Title 26 IRS CODE

"You are the one bringing the foreign products into the United States!" Under the Law of Merchants (import/export law) you owe a duty or excise tax upon those products you bring into the United States. Put in another way, anyone who brings in, or deals with foreign merchandise is subject to an indirect excise tax on that activity. However, lawful money, gold and silver coin and certificate does not exist. You can't use lawful money (gold and silver coin) to pay the excise taxes upon the foreign products (FRNs) that you bring in, because lawful money was removed by the Federal government. Yet you are certainly in contract with a foreign corporation, the Federal Reserve Bank. You are in transaction with its products. Hence, you are compelled to give an equivalent value in the foreign product (FRNs), as the excise, in lieu of paying actual gold, silver or their certificates for the tax owed.

26 CFR § 1.861-8 (together with the various statutes of Subchapter N) shows that taxable "sources of income" do apply to the activities of international or foreign commerce. The questions for you are: "Does one engage in international or foreign commerce when he/she exchanges his labor for the foreign and privately owned products called Federal Reserve Notes by cashing or depositing his/her check at a bank? Does he/she engage in international or foreign commerce when he/she buys a 'thing' with the Federal Reserve Notes, which the notes themselves are in international law? Does he/she engage in foreign/international commerce by transacting with checks that are backed by Federal Reserve notes and processed and accounted for by the

Federal Reserve Banks? Is not transacting in the foreign product a deceitful means to compel you into a commercial activity, which would make you subject to pay taxes upon the use of the foreign product? How many of those products have come into and gone out of your household in your yearly transactions? Even your weekly transactions. How many of those products (FRNs) have you brought into your house at the end of the year, which products are also known as your gross income? Does this reek of a scheme that only a malignantly vile and greedy Bea$t could have invented to deceive you? Wouldn't you agree that if the lien is in place upon every Federal Reserve Note you have <u>used</u> in your entire life that the lien now carries over into everything you have purchased or sold? These are only some of the questions you may be asking yourself. DISCLAIMER: We are not stating that any tax is legal or illegal, lawful or unlawful. These questions and their answers are for the reader to decide. We merely want to present the knowledge that the Mark of the Bea$t is upon all things. It's upon all people, including you, your loved ones, relatives, neighbors, and the derelict under the bridge!

Contract = Lien of FRB   The contract for painting your house – or any other agreement you enter with a neighbor or anyone else where you pay with Federal Reserve Notes instead of trading labor or paying with substance (gold or silver) – is liened for $1,500.00. That contract now belongs to the Federal Reserve Bank who is the Primary Party in interest. In other words, the FRB owns the contract!

U $\leftrightarrow$ FRB $\leftrightarrow$ N   You and your neighbor are each dealing directly with the FRB, the primary party of interest to the contract, because it holds the hidden lien for $1,500.00.

Painted House   The new paint on the house now belongs to the FRB because that became the security for the lien. That is because you did not make an actual payment in gold, silver, or their certificates. Moreover, you are paying your mortgage in Federal Reserve Notes. So, in addition, your house itself belongs to the FRB.

Debtor

Since you do not own anything, nor can you pay for anything, the liens carry from the note to the very 'things' they have been used for. You now are a debtor that cannot pay your debts. Legally, you are insolvent. That makes you the chattel of the Bea$t! His Mark, the Mark of the Bea$t is upon your hand, and upon your head! Are you one with unalienable rights or subject to the Bea$t while you are using the property of the Bea$t? The mark of the Bea$t is upon your head! Have you not become its property (chattel) regardless of whether or not you believe you have unalienable rights? Is it not a blessing for all of us to be prosperous, and with free will, possessing Life, Liberty, Happiness, and our own Property?

Now, have the invisible powers of the IRS been made visible? The IRS is the collection entity for the contract in Admiralty. You were tricked into that contract by using $limed product, product that you can never own, or pay the lien on.

Please reread the prophesy to absolutely bring home the message:

***And that no man might buy or sell, save he that had the mark, or the name of the beast, or the number of his name.* Rev. 13:17-18**

Can you buy or sell without the mark of the hidden lien? No! Did it pass into your right hand? Yes! Does not this mark brand the property by deceit, trickery, lies and beguilement? Yes! Does not the $lime of hidden liens transfer to the next human soul? Yes! Is there not a specific name owning the hypothecation? Yes, the FRB. Is deliberate deceit not a vile act?

CHAPTER 19

RAMIFICATIONS OF THE MARK

"The real menace of our Republic is the invisible government which like a giant octopus sprawls its slimy legs over our cities states and nation. At the head is a small group of banking houses generally referred to as 'international bankers.' This little coterie... run our government for their own selfish ends. It operates under cover of a self-created screen...[and] seizes...our executive officers... legislative bodies... schools... courts... newspapers and every agency created for the public protection."
(John F. Hylan, Mayor of New York City from 1918 to 1925)

With the veil of deceit lifted, you have now discovered that you don't own anything. You are using another entity's property in all your contracts. The foundation of liberty is the ownership of property. Without property that is exclusively yours, how can you enter into any sort of contract without the permission of the lien holder? Simply put, you can't!

Furthermore, your use of FRNs identifies you as a debtor in use of the creditor's property. You, and every contract into which you enter with its property, are subject to its terms and conditions.

In 1933, President Franklin Delano Roosevelt not only conspired and stole the gold of every American, he stole their personal and real property. And further, because of his acts, presently your personal and real property have been stolen. He also replaced it with instruments marked by the bea$t. You were sold into insolvency. Remember, when one is insolvent he is literally owned by the creditor, who could jail the debtor. People have been sold into slavery throughout history. We don't have physical debtor prisons anymore, or do we? (Please see clarification note at end of chapter) Could you be in a debtor's prison without bars, a prison with the *illusion* of freedom? Let's examine that concept.

Within a few years of the gold confiscation and replacement by marked debt notes, came laws of the kind never seen before in America. Roosevelt's New Deal, allegedly for recovery of the Depression, created agency after agency, board after board, license after license. Occupations, which are your common law right to work, suddenly required a license. A license is permission by the state to do that which otherwise would be illegal.

> Bouvier's Law Dictionary: **LICENSE**, contracts. *A right given by some competent authority to do an act, which without such authority would be illegal. The instrument or writing which secures this right, is also called a license.*

How did cutting hair (cosmetology), performed for centuries as a common law right, suddenly become illegal? Or ministering to the sick (medicine, nursing, chiropractic, naturopathy)? Or burying the dead (undertaker)?

A marriage, a birth, a death -- these were all recorded in the family's Holy Bible, not in the County Court House records. There was no NEED to record them there, because they dealt with real people (form and substance).

How did even marriage come to need state permission by license? Previously it was a holy contract entered into before God in a house of worship. How did the spiritual product of this union, children, need registration with the state? The answer is that we have become the chattel property of some entity (the Federal Reserve Bank), requiring registration and permission.

Why did you suddenly need state permission to travel the roads? Suddenly, to serve your fellow man, you needed a license or registration from the state (professional license). Coming soon is a national ID card and gun registration, and possibly gun confiscation.

By understanding the facts presented, you should now recognize that you have become a debtor. You no longer have any unalienable rights. You now only have the privileges licensed to you by your creditor. You became his property by the invisible mark. Virtually every aspect of your life is now regulated by the state. You even need permission to remodel your house. Do you see why? It is not your house. There is a hidden lien on it. What did you use to acquire it? The property of the creditor! The creditor has its interest to protect. You became subject to rules and regulations no different than a prisoner. Only you weren't placed behind physical bars. Your bars are invisible.

In 1933, the U.S. government went insolvent. It too then became a debtor subject to the creditor. But, you weren't told. We the People don't have any idea what the terms and conditions of that Chapter 11 bankruptcy included. But the evidence leaves a clear trail. The government became the agent of collection for the creditor. The debt was dumped on us. We were collectively beguiled into a debtor's status. The creditor worked the terms and conditions through the government. If the creditor did this openly, we would not be beguiled. But the cruelest and most unconscionable effect from this act is that it is perpetual!

Roosevelt, by stealing our gold, lifted us out of our common law unalienable rights and placed us into commercial law where there are only privileges. In common law, you are presumed innocent until proven guilty beyond reasonable doubt. In commercial law, or administrative law, when the agency comes after you, they don't have to prove you are guilty to seize or penalize. You are presumed guilty until you prove your innocence, which is impossible to do. That's because their attack is based only on an action by you which did not necessarily cause damage. You are cited by an officer of the agency. The agency will accept unsworn hearsay evidence to condemn you. You are demanded to surrender this "property" (FRNs). It can be forcibly taken from you without the protected right of trial by jury of your peers prior to property seizure. Remember, that unalienable right was enshrined in the Magna Charta and is a lawful due process right. In administrative law, property is taken from you (seized) without lawful authority. You often have to prove a negative, a virtual impossibility. If they say that you did something, and you did not, how do you prove that you did not?

You have no right to have the entire nature of the action weighed by a jury. Often you have to pay what is exacted (demanded of you) before you can utter a word. When you are on board the ship in Admiralty law, if the captain says you are guilty, you are guilty. Hop on and walk the plank! Many medical doctors have lost their ability to earn a living. What was their "crime"? They were delivering health services that the state agency (medical board) did not believe in. This often occurs without a patient's complaint, even if a patient has asked for the service and improved. It includes patients who were cured from the same.

Do you actually think that you are in the status of possessing Rights rather than privileges? Do you consider yourself a citizen of the United States? Let's look at the 14th amendment briefly.

> 1. All persons born or naturalized in the United States, and subject [Editor's note, "inferior status"] to the jurisdiction thereof, are citizens of the United States and of the State wherein they reside. No State shall make or enforce any law which shall abridge the privileges or immunities of citizens of the United States… (Emphasis and brackets added).

Prior to the 14th Amendment, Americans were Sovereigns without subjects (Chisholm v Georgia, previously cited, Chapter 9). After the 14th Amendment, Americans were no longer their own Sovereign, but became subjects of the U.S. Government.

Note, this amendment was passed in 1868 to protect the newly "freed" slaves after the civil war ended in 1865. Further note that the recently "freed" and black "citizens of the United States" were not given unalienable Rights. How could a corporate entity (The United States) grant unalienable rights? Those come from the Creator (Declaration of Independence). The 14th amendment citizens were granted only "privileges or immunities." A great teacher said, "You can't serve two masters." Serve your Creator and you are blessed with unalienable Rights that are granted by your Creator. Serve the corporate United States and you will be granted mere privileges. And why did this happen? Look to clause 4 of said amendment:

> 4.   *The validity of the public debt of the United States, authorized by law, including debts incurred for payment of pensions and bounties for services in suppressing insurrection or rebellion,* **shall not be questioned**. *(emphasis added)*

The <u>amended</u> Constitution openly admits that the nation was in debt. Debts can't be questioned. They are a contract. If you are a citizen of the United States, you can't question the debt. You are subject [inferior status] to its jurisdiction. Before the Civil War, slaves were the commercial property of their masters. After the Civil War, their legal status was not changed; they merely were subject to a new master, the United States. Though under the illusion they were free, they had no <u>political</u> status (state-recognized rights) from 1865 to 1868. The amendment granted *legal status*. *"Legal status"* is a status pendant upon the law of man. Hence, it may be amended or repealed by men. "Legal status" did/does not, however, recognize the *natural status* (from the Creator) that all men were endowed with, as acknowledged by the Declaration of Independence. This Creator-endowed status may NOT be amended or repealed by men. But, the *legal status* tied their "privileges and immunities" to the laws of the corporate United States rather than to their Creator. They were now subject to the jurisdiction of the corporate U.S. rather than the jurisdiction of a plantation. You and the rest of us have unwittingly also walked into this inferior status of the government plantation. How? When you entered into international commerce, you have subjected yourself to U.S. jurisdiction under the commerce clause! You can't question the debt, now placed on you. You have no unalienable rights, only privileges. Have you been beguiled?

Oh, but you think you have recourse in the courts. Well in the next chapter we'll see just whose courts they are.

Notes: Wikipedia does tell us that there are remaining states with physical debtor's prisons. There is also increasing incarceration for debt involving child support.

"A **debtors' prison** is a prison for those who are unable to pay a debt. Prior to the mid 19th century debtors' prisons were a common way to deal with unpaid debt."

United States
"In 1833 the United States reduced the practice of imprisonment for debts at the federal level. Most states followed suit. It is still possible, however, to be incarcerated for debt: debts of fraud, child-support, alimony, or release fines can land a citizen in jail or prison, or prevent one's release."

Chapter 20

The New Courts

"The system of banking we have both equally and ever reprobated. I contemplate it as a blot left in all our constitutions, which, if not covered, will end in their destruction, which is already hit by the gamblers in corruption, and is sweeping away in its progress the fortunes and morals of our citizens."
(Thomas Jefferson, 3rd U.S. President)

The original courts of the nation were called Courts of the United States. Their accounts were exclusively kept in lawful gold and silver coin according to the Coinage Act section 20 (Appendix F):

> *"And be it further enacted, That the money of account of the United States shall be expressed in dollars (or fractions of it)...... and that all accounts in the public offices and all proceedings in the courts of the United States shall be kept and had in conformity to this regulation." [Dollars were defined as a specific weight of precious metal]*

United States money of accounts is, to this day, precious metal, which is coin minted by said act. In 1933, gold money was stolen from the people. (After 1964, silver coin disappeared as well.) The courts were in trouble. Under law, they had to transact in real money. So what did the tricksters do? They beguiled us into a new "court" by illusion.

If you were blindfolded, and walked into a court, when the wrappings were removed and the money argued over and paid over was Yen, you would know that you were in a Japanese court. You can identify the sovereign of the court by the money used. If you pay the court in rubles, it would be a Russian court.

A new court was created in 1938, a *mirror image*, called the United States District Court (28 USC§132(a)). The new statute did not specify the money of accounts for that court. That would have been a visible dead give away. But go into that court and see what product is used! The sovereign on the currency used is not the United States. It is the Federal Reserve Bank. So whose court are you in? The creditor's! Now, do you wonder why you can't question the debt? Do you wonder why there are summary proceedings where your unalienable common law right to present all of the facts is ignored? Do you wonder why the judge can arbitrarily exclude evidence to the jury? It is a commercial court owned by the creditor!!!! If you were the creditor and your debtor walked into your proceedings, would you treat him any differently? The Creditor, ***as the Bea$t***, seeks what property is his.

We offer you absolute proof. Here is a true story a rational man may not believe. The government sued a man for an alleged tax debt of over $1 million to reduce it to judgment (USDC Northern District of California 03-109 CIV). Of course, there was no way for him to question the allegation. The United States asked for summary judgment. That fits. That means that the man would be denied any ability to defend. Remember, an IRS collection action is Admiralty. There had to be a contract. There is no defense when you "break" a contract.

The defendant did argue and presented an unexpected remedy and defense. It was the most important defense that he had. His defense came from the common law. He presented a $5.00 (and NOT a $5.00 FRN) pre 1933 gold coin and lodged it into the accounts of the court attached to a contract for payment and extinguishment of the entire debt. We believe that he is the first and only man to have done this, since the great heist of 1933, which stole the gold.

The United States remained silent on the claim of payment and extinguishment. It had a firm duty according to the rules of court to respond. It defaulted. By all rules and practices of that same court, the case should have then been dismissed. Why? There was an accord and satisfaction. (This term means that a debtor actually pays the debt with form and substance rather than with form only for payment of the alleged debt. That part is called the accord. When the creditor accepts it, that is the satisfaction. The debt is extinguished by offer and acceptance). In this case, the silence of the United States was acquiescence. Acquiescence is a principle in law, in which, by your silence, you have accepted the thing you have received. During the course of the case the United States remained silent for the entire case concerning this payment.

In oral arguments, the judge took notice of the gold coin payment. He asked the U.S. attorney how he values the coin. The US attorney stated, "I believe it's dollar for dollar?" The defendant responded, "There is no place in the federal code that provides for a conversion of lawful money to Federal Reserve Notes." *In fact, a conversion table does not exist in laws of the United States of America!*

Now hold on a moment. Only the Congress can weigh and value the coin. And Congress did value the coin - five dollars gold weight. Was it not treasonable to the United States Constitution for the court to ask the Executive branch how it values the coin? Should have not this United States court recognized its own money of accounts of this country?

A summary decision that should have taken two days to determine took well over 6 months. The judge did award summary judgment of the total sum in excess of $1M. But he left a trail as to how he was able to skirt the issue of actual payment. In a footnote at the end, he admonished the defendant (not the U.S. attorney he questioned in court) for not providing the "monetary value, if any" of the coin. He further ordered the clerk of the court to return the lawful gold coin of the United States of America to the defendant.

Astonishing, out of one side of his mouth, the court's judge says that the man had a debt. Out of the other side, the court's judge orders a payment the man made to be returned.

How did this happen?

Even the Bea$t has rules and principles he has to live by. He cannot claim what is not his. He can't grab what did not come to him voluntarily, though gained by deceit. Neither can the creditor. The coin was not debt. It was never "taxable income". The coin did not have the hidden lien as the FRN. Remember, the tax is upon the taxable income. The coin never had such vile status, since it was never an international liened commercial instrument. It was not property (a product) that could be accepted by the current government in any way since it was never the subject of an excise tax. It was never the product of the creditor directly or indirectly. Moreover, the creditor had no secured interest in the coin.

The courts are debtors' courts. They adjudicate debtors and debtors' instruments. The courts cannot see anything else. The coin had no value in a system where the illusion of "money" is debt (IOUs), and all litigants do is exchange debt. There must be value for an accord. The judge negated all the value to the lawful gold coin of the United States of America. (Of course the lawful gold coin had no value in a monetary system that pushes debtor instruments, the FRNs.) He thereby negated the accord and satisfaction and treated it as if it never happened, or that it was frivolous. Doing so relieved the requirement that the U.S. had to respond to the fact that the debt was actually paid by gold! With no alleged value to the offer, the offer was "frivolous" and could be ignored. That means there was essentially no offer and the whole offer proceeding could be ignored, as if it didn't occur. OF PARAMOUNT IMPORTANCE, note, the court did determine that all lawful gold coins of the

United States of America have NO value to the commercial jurisdiction. Think about the ramifications of this and how you may apply this principle to your needs.

POINT: The "conversion" table between lawful gold coins of the United States of America and Federal Reserve Notes needs to be understood.

When you are thinking of a "conversion" table between lawful gold coins and Federal Reserve Notes, we would ask that you consider this kind of table in the light of the math you once learned in the school system. If you remember the positive and negative integers, you will recall that the negative numbers were on the left of the zero, and the positive integers were on the right as follows: …

(To infinity ← … Negative Integers)   (Positive Integers … → to infinity)

…, −9, −8, −7, −6, −5, −4, −3, −2, −1, 0, 1, 2, 3, 4, 5, 6, 7, 8, 9,…

Hence, in this matter of money, the positive integers would be represented by the Lawful gold coins of the United States of America because they have both form and substance. The negative integers would be represented by the Federal Reserve Notes because they are in form only, and lack substance. They are purely abstractions (make believe). Now we would like you to think of apples in place of the coins for our example concerning positive and negative integers. See the following questions and answers concerning how positive and negative integers apply to exampling apples:

Question 1: If you have five apples (positive integer) from your neighbor's tree, how many apples do you actually have?

Answer: "I <u>actually</u> have five apples."

Question 2: If you ate every one of the five apples, including their cores, how many apples do you now have?

Answer: "I would have no apples."

Question 3: Now, with no apples, if you (pretend to) eat five apples including their cores, do you now have minus five apples (negative integer (−5)?

Answer: "If I have eaten every one of the imaginary apples including their cores I have minus five apples (−5)."

In the above three questions and answers we have come through the positive integers to the negative integers. We came from having five actual apples to having five imaginary apples that no longer exist.

Question 4: Do the five positive apples equal the five negative apples,

or (+5 = −5)?

Answer: " No, actual apples cannot equal imaginary apples. There cannot be a conversion table to make the actual apples equal to the imaginary apples."

Now let's ask similar questions but let's substitute the real and imaginary apples for both the Lawful gold coins of the United States of America (gold coin) and the Federal Reserve Notes (FRNs). We will place the gold coins on the positive side of the integers because the coins have both *form* and *substance (gold shaped in a coin)*. We will place the FRNs on the negative side of the integers because the FRNs have only *form,* meaning that nothing is backing them (created almost out of thin air).

Question 1: If you have five gold coins in your treasure chest, how many gold coins do you actually have?

Answer: "I <u>actually</u> have five gold coins."

Question 2: If you spent every one of the five gold coins, how many gold coins do you now have in your treasure chest?

Answer: " I would have zero or no gold coins in my treasure chest."

Question 3: If you spent (subtract) another five gold coins starting from zero, meaning you do not have any coins, do you now have minus five gold coins? (This minus figure or imaginary figure represents the Federal Reserve Note. It is a debt and falls in the minus integers, in contrast to the gold coins, which fall into the positive integers.)

Answer: "If I have spent another five gold coins I have five negative gold coins (FRNs)."

Question 4: Do the five positive gold coins equal the five negative gold coins (FRNs) or $(+5 = -5)$?

Answer: "No, real gold coins cannot equal imaginary gold coins (FRNs). There cannot be a conversion table to make the real equal to the imaginary."

Last Question:

Question 5: Between Lawful gold coins and Federal Reserve Notes, let's say you can pick between a $20.00 Lawful gold coin of the United States of America, which is still the money of account of this country, and a $20.00 Federal Reserve Note. Which one would you choose?

Answer: If you chose the Federal Reserve Note, then the authors would like to do business with you. We would ask that you exchange your Lawful $20.00 Gold Coin of the United States for our Federal Reserve Notes. We will trade you a $20.00 FRN, plus we will pay you an additional $100.00 of FRNs for the time you spent getting the coin. How can you lose with a good deal like this?

Back to the true story, a few pages back: The defendant took his case all the way to the Supreme Court. In his petition for review, he told the court that if the case was not reversed, it would be tantamount to sustaining the finding of the lower court that lawful coined money would be invisible to the government in the payment of the debt. Lawful money would fall out of its grasp entirely. The court denied review, which amounted to approving the decision of the lower court. If the court/government could not see the coin, how can the government tax it? How can the government impose a tax on us if we transacted our affairs within common law using actual and lawful gold money, which the government (by its courts) has acquiesced it cannot "see"?

There is double proof (the coin and the judges oath – see appendix C) – that the courts in front of us are not Courts of the United States. In Appendix C you will see a nearly imperceptible alteration in the "judge's" oath of office. They don't recognize lawful and gold money of the United States or the (Common) Law of the United States. It recognizes only the opposite. So whose court is it? They are the courts of the creditor. It even ordered the coin's return when a debt was adjudicated! The court only sees the debt notes (FRNs) of the creditor (the FRB), its master. "You cannot serve two masters." Whose court is it? The creditor's! And, it is not a court under your God. In fact, your God is not allowed into these courts. But monkeys are! (Scope's Monkey/evolution trial).

The beguiling is now lifted for you. The U.S. District Court is a bankruptcy court enforcing the rules, regulations, and privileges granted by the creditor to its debtors (chattel). It can only see form, not substance. It is working solely with the negative (debt) integers. Is it the agent of the Bea$t? When you get hauled into that court are your unalienable Sovereign rights there? Or is there another master (FRB) vs. you, the chattel?

Now you know about the "money" (FRNs) that supposedly balances "law" on the scales of justice in the current courts. Consider what you are faced with in these courts by understanding the following scale of justice we have today. On one side of the scale is your debt; you are the insolvent. On the opposite side is your creditor's agent enforcing all of the rules and regulations upon you, the insolvent.

Debt Notes

Creditor's Enforcer

Chapter 21

The Theft of your Substance

"It is said that our paper is as good as silver, because we may have silver for it at the bank where it issues. This is not true. One, two, or three persons might have it; but a general application would soon exhaust their vaults, and leave a ruinous proportion of their paper in its intrinsic worthless form."
(Thomas Jefferson, 3rd U.S. President)

What Jefferson said is exactly why we went belly up. The bea$t distributed far more phony pieces of paper than was backed by substance. The vaults were exhausted. We are now also using worthless ruinous paper.

Let's look at this precisely on point. Gold is land, portable land. It's extracted from the ground. It's "value" remained fixed for over 150 years. One ounce represented twenty dollars. When FDR stole our gold, he returned a $20 worthless note attached with liens. Within two weeks, the government raised the price of gold to $35 paper currency per ounce. Hence, those who were warehousing the gold made an overnight profit of 75% (in paper). You know who was warehousing it **(the FRB)**! A profit overnight of 75%. Doesn't that violate the banker's new definition of usury? Their new definition is "unreasonable interest" (profit)! But they are the bankers! They are now remaking all the rules and redefining age-old terms.

Suppose you worked hard and had stuffed 10,000 dollars in gold certificates in your mattress in 1933. Before the theft, at $20 per ounce, you had the right to 500 ounces of gold. You actually live to a ripe old age and in 2008, need that money to survive. Those certificates are now worth exactly $10,000 FRNs. With the world waking up to the banking deception, that $10,000 will bring only about ten ounces of gold in 2008. Your nest egg was wiped out by 95%. The bankers couldn't control gold. They can control the product they print and which product (FRNs) steals from you! One 20 dollar one ounce gold coin in 1933 would buy a gun or a fine suit. It still has the same value to get that same gun or suit today. Does the $20 FRN? Have you been tricked? Isn't that what is happening on a similar scale to folks who saved up a nest egg only to see more printed debt notes (FRNs) dilute what they think they have? Isn't that what's happening now to people on fixed income Social Security? Whatever illusory value it has is getting eaten away like a cancer.

We realize after a lifetime of brainwashing by the government, you still might be confused. You still may think that the FRNs you carry are yours after you pay your income tax. Think again. We offer you yet more evidence that you already know. Try leaving the country with more than $10,000 (FRNs or other negotiable instruments) of what you think is yours. Try walking into a bank and withdrawing more than $10,000 of what you think is yours. You know that if you move more than $10,000 FRNs in any fashion to anyone, you must report it. The creditor (bea$t) simply wants to keep track of the bulk of the obligations due him.

After all, they are his property. He gets to set the rules on your use of his property.

Now why might the bea$t have concocted up the fraudulent war on drugs? Do you really believe that he cares about someone using drugs? Or is it for control? Is it to make you think that the reporting of these sums is to track down criminals? Indeed it *is* to track criminals. But the criminal they are tracking is you. Remember, to be a debtor is a crime. You are free on terms and conditions. The so called "Patriot Act" (P.L. 107-56, 115 Stat. 272 (2001)) wiped out most of the few loopholes people still retained to avoid the creditor knowing everything about them. Do you think the drug "wars" are really in place to nab drug merchants? Or is it an excuse to track every movement of $10,000 cash by ordinary people like you?

Now, try leaving the country with $1,000,000 face value pre 1933 gold dollars. You certainly can! There is no restriction on real money unliened by the creditor. The government can't see these coins at all! The restriction is on fictional representations of money such as currency and all monetary instruments (NOT MONEY!), which is everything $limed by the Creditor (**Bea$t**).

FRNs are taxed upon your receipt of them as "income". Can you still tell us that after this tax that the FRNs are really yours? Well, now consider inheritance taxes. Try leaving your children your house, stocks and other assets you stashed away AFTER paying income tax. In the case of estate taxes, it should be obvious to you by now the mechanism of the tax. Consider the true stories of families own-ing land for generations. Due to the fraud of the system, the "value" in FRNs inflates exponentially. Let say that the landholder dies. The family must sell their land to pay the estate tax, say of $4,000,000 on property that might have cost perhaps $100 in gold years ago. Even if you are not transferring FRNs held in an account, the creditor gets his rake in the property transfer. Why? Because all your prop-erty is liened, and the value is inflated to so called market value in the worthless notes. If it were really yours, how could the Creditor ever interfere with you giving what you will to your family? Clearly, the assets are not yours, even if you paid income taxes at the highest rate on what you accumulated. Inheritance and gift taxes are on the activ-ity (excise, which in this instance is the ***transfer*** of the FRN value to others) regarding the FRN commodity and every-thing is $limed (liened) in the transfers. Remember, you are chattel. You possess property by privilege only. You don't own anything. You only have a "certificate" of title, not the actual title to a house or car. Т̃һ℮ӯ **Own It All (Including You!)** To leave for your children the liened property you possess costs your estate an excise tax for the privilege.

We certainly hope that we have satisfactorily driven home the point.

CHAPTER 22

THE FINAL SOLUTION

"The best slave is the slave who thinks he is free."
(Anonymous)

Let's look at your "freedoms" and liberties in the light of the above quote.

In the common law, here is a partial list of your Unalienable Rights:

* indicates a specific listing in the Constitution

*** indicates specific mention in the Declaration Independence

      1.   contract*
      2.   Liberty which includes travel***
      3.   your children
      4.   religion*
      5.   your labor
      6.   marriage
      7.   privacy*
      8.   Property, personal and real *
      9.   protection from unwarranted search and seizure*

10. trial where the jury weighs the law as well as the facts
11. plenary due process *
12. speech*
13. assembly*
14. Redress of grievance*
15. Life***
16. protect your property
17. post offices*
18. Keep and bear arms *

Our alleged government insists that we are a free country, that we have liberties, and that we should export our notion of freedom around the world. Let's examine one by one.

Contract* – No right. There is a creditor between you and every one you contract with. The creditor takes his share of the transaction impairing the obligation. A debtor cannot contract without the creditor. Everything you think you own is impaired by the $lime of the hypothecated lien. Therefore, in all your transactions, no matter what, there are at least two other hidden parties involved.

They are "The United States of America," whose obligation you are using, and the "Federal Reserve Bank," the real party in interest. You can't even barter with your labor since you are chattel. The creditor wants and has claim to a piece of everything that you do to repay the debt.

Liberty *** Have you unalienable rights to Liberty? If so, why are you required to get permission from the state to operate your "private" car on the public roads? Why do you need a passport to enter your own country? And why is the government relentlessly pressing for a national ID card? What happened to the Liberty of marrying without state license?

Religion* Churches have become one with the FRB. They are using its monetary instruments instead of the treasury of man's labor (gold and/or silver). As such, they are subject to the rules and regulations of the FRB or they will lose their tax exempt status. How did the state get to impose a tax upon a house of worship? How did the state get to force the house of worship to incorporate and be a fictional creature of the state instead of a creation of God? Do you have freedom to marry without the permission (license) of the state? Did you know that the Supreme Court has ruled that Indians can no longer use the ceremonial mushrooms in their religious practices that they have used for centuries?

Here's your ultimate proof:

With Executive Order 13397, dated March 7, 2006, the President has turned churches that accept Faith Based Funds into a government agency with spy type reporting requirement to the Dept. of Homeland Security. Churches themselves are now incorporated into and literally one with the Bea$t simply by making use of his marked property. Your church, using $limed debt notes has unwittingly been marked by the Bea$t and has unwittingly become its agent. Congress has replaced your God with the Bea$t.

Children. – Within the common law, you are the absolute custodian of your children until age 18, when they reach majority. If that is so, why do you have to register with the state your offspring? How does the state get to impose vaccinations on your child? How does the state get to forcibly remove the child from you if you don't agree with medical care demanded by state licensed doctors? Here's your answer. You are chattel yourself for the crime of being a debtor. Please look in the Appendix B for a copy of the California birth registration form. Note that the declarant is "Parent or other Informant". You as a parent are declaring yourself to be an *informant* by these beguiling words. An *informant* [4] is one who tells the authorities of a crime. Indeed there is a crime that has been committed. The appearance of another debtor, who must be registered. You are never given the original of the birth certificate. The information thereon goes to the Department of Commerce! See Appendix B. Why does birth information and registration go the United States Commerce Department? Evidence dear reader, evidence that you and your children are mere chattel in commerce. Since the creditor thinks that forced vaccines will protect his chattel (property), he imposes it.

Privacy* The word does not specifically appear in the Constitution, but the Supreme Court has held that the people

---

4   **Informer** – A person who informs or prefers an accusation against another, whom he suspects of a violation of a penal statute. Black's Law Dictionary – Revised Fourth Edition, page 919

have a right to privacy. But as a debtor, do you have a right to privacy? Note that your tax form asks you to reveal just about every aspect of your finances. It also asks for many things not necessarily related to income. Coming soon, hot out of Congress will be the ability of the IRS to grab all your credit card history. Any thoughts of privacy still? Of course they can "legally" look at your credit card transactions. You are using the property of the bea$t in these transactions and "payments". They are just looking out for what is theirs. With this information handed to the bea$t, the average American will have told him everything by self confession. The government can and does secretly listen in on your phone conversations legally in order to "find terrorists".

Property *: This unalienable right is found in state constitutions. However, if you still possessed that unalienable right, would you need permission from the county to remodel your home, even if fully "paid" for? Could the government charge you with a crime and seize everything you own before you were convicted? It's happening! You don't own anything. 𝕿𝖍𝖊𝖞 **Own Everything!**

It's all liened commercial property! That's why you don't have the power to protect by force what you think is your property. That power is left in the hands of the creditor's "law" enforcers.

Search and seizure * Seizure is Admiralty. All search warrants for your property on the land are Admiralty as well. You are being searched on the basis of an international contract. Your property is seized on that basis as well.

Trial by jury* Indeed you are tried by a jury of your peers. They are all debtors. As such, the jury cannot weigh the law since there is no (common) law. There are only rules and regulations respecting the chattel of the creditor. The judge tells the jury what it must do to weigh the rules of the creditor against the facts.

Plenary due process* You are a debtor. You are in an Admiralty court based on a contract that you violated. You get the due process dictated by the captain of the ship. It's called summary procedure where he determines what facts are relevant before you walk the plank. You do not have the common law due process rights of one who can pay debt. The judge filters the evidence he wants the jury to hear. In common law you once could present anything and everything you wanted to the jury.

Speech* Alas, we know that there are many in the health industry who are fined or jailed for making health claims that the FDA didn't like. Did you know that the FDA, like the Nazis, has burned books about healing? Aside from the burning of some communist materials in the 1950's, it's the only agency ever in the USA to have done so, and has done so repeatedly! (See the following websites)

http://findarticles.com/p/articles/mi_m0FKA/is_12_60/ai_53421299

http://www.orgonelab.org/fda.htm

http://wiki.answers.com/Q/What_is_the_history_of_book_burning

www.wrf.org/men-women-medicine/spectrochrome-**dinshah**-ghadiali.php

When you are dealing in commerce, you are subject to regulation. Anything that touches a FRN is in commerce and is subject to commercial speech restrictions. Now you know how the Federal Trade Commission and the FDA rip people apart. But those torn asunder never knew! If you connect any product, book, or service to a FRN, it enters commerce. Speech regarding an item connected to FRN's can be regulated! But consider this. In the common law, a man can call you any name he will. He can carry any sign he wants. He can do just about anything as long as he doesn't interfere with your Liberty, such as striking you. But what if he burned a cross on "his" property? He can't do that anymore. This is not to condone such activities. It's merely to mention that the activities are nothing more than free speech and expression, now restricted.

Assembly* Does the KKK have anymore the right to assemble and do a cross burning, no matter what you think of them? Do you have the right to assemble in front of an abortion clinic in protest? Why of course not. You are interfering with commerce, as would be the KKK.

Redress of grievance* Ask the group We the People (http://www.givemeliberty.org) about redress of grievance. They have gone to court to demand that alleged right to force the government to tell them what the taxing statute is. The courts have turned them down. Whoops, debtors have no right to petition the creditor for anything. Does chattel get to petition the owner?

Life*** Let's look again at California. A minor child in California has far more rights to terminate a pregnancy without her parent's knowledge or consent than her 40 year old mother has to treat her breast cancer the way she wants to in the "privacy" of her doctor's office. The unborn debtor has no right to life. Doctors and patients are at the mercy of the creditor. Coming soon to America from Europe is a world trade commercial agreement called Codex. It will subject commerce in nutritional supplements to draconian regulations. These will eliminate many of your favorite supplements, and limit the dose on others, or make prescriptions out of them. Already in many countries the maximum amount of vitamin C in a tablet is less than 200mg, compared to 5 times that here (America).

The creditor picks and chooses through the Food Drug Administration (FDA) which chemical treatments will be allowed for the chattel to treat the diseases the chattel are allowed to get. Diseases you are allowed to get? Yes. Just look at the coding after your doctor visits. If what you have doesn't fit the parameters of what the edicts the government has laid down for diagnoses, there won't be reimbursement. And for treatment? There could be a cure overseas for your disease. But try getting it through the FDA controlled U.S. Customs. And you think that you have a right to Life?

Post Offices* Have you not noticed? There is no "Post Office". It's the "Postal Service". Another bait and switch mirror image. The Postal Service thanks you for your "business". You have "purchased" postage with commercial notes. That places everything you mail at the mercy of commercial mail statutes. At least one physician has been convicted criminally for the fraud of using the mail to bill for alternative medicine. The Post Office was for communication between people. It is now a commercial activity. Speaking of this, what is being used to pay for internet services and the world-wide-web? Can you now see the writing on the wall for legal means to regulate the internet as well? The communication lines belong to the bea$t, just like the Postal Service.

Keep and bear arms* Just pay attention to every effort by the government to grab your guns. The Founders recognized that the final and ultimate protection for the People from government was/is their personal weapons. One of the first acts of the Nazis in Germany was to strip people of their guns, leaving them utterly helpless.

CHAPTER 23

SUMMARY

"Competition is sin."
(John D. Rockefeller)

Please go back to the prologue and read the alternate example. We have shown you in real life that that scenario has happened. It was not a religious figure fresh out of the fires and in the light of day that beguiled or branded you with his red hot iron. He didn't come to your door either. That would be too obvious. Treachery works in darkness. Greed came to the government as men dressed in suits. They bore pieces of paper that lured those in power. Their offer was a promised end to vicious economic cycles that they themselves deliberately created. The catch was that the government would impose upon the people their $limed pieces of paper (currency). Government officials sold their souls. It wasn't you. It was your government that sold out. The $lime of their sell out quickly marked you as well. Not long after the bankers set up shop, the economy crashed and burned. Our government defaulted. In the aftermath of the destruction the bankrupt government was taken over in receivership. It then compelled us to use commercial debt notes. We were not given notice or choice. Nor were we, in any way, made aware as to the terms, conditions, and agreements that our "public servants" made with the creditor men in black. But what is clear is that those pieces of paper are compelled upon us. Compelled into commerce, you are taxed on the use of those $limed notes. Your labor is literally stolen from you for using these notes, rather than gold. Even worse, what you are permitted to keep is liened. The FRNs carry debt. They have marked you with an invisible lien on every aspect of your life. You cannot buy or sell without the mark of the Bea$t, the invisible lien. The removal of substance for payment has occurred worldwide. There may not be any countries left with gold backed currency, leaving virtually the entire world population in the same boat under the international bankers.

And that no man might buy or sell, save he that had the mark (the invisible lien)*, or the name of the beast* (one of the myriad names of the same entity - various international banks such as the FRB)*, or the number of his name* (notes or credit-debit accounting system of debt). (The international bankers have pushed for a one world currency wherein the various names of the same Bea$t will be reduced to one name). The person you give it (the liened commodity) to is likewise marked and his labor stolen as well. You are transferring the mark in every transaction you make, most assuredly with your right hand. You cannot buy or sell without using instruments in the "name" or "number" (denomination) of the "Bea$t" as the prophecy predicts.

You, yourself, have become mere chattel. As a debtor or chattel, you possess government (creditor) granted privileges, not Sovereign rights – our lawful birthright.

You have been compelled out of the honest common law and your unalienable rights. In the latter, you were Sovereign. You have been cast into a jurisdiction of the Bea$t. Greed *is* "the "Bea$t." In that jurisdiction, the Bea$t can forcibly take from you at will by hearsay accusation only. Yet when you present written claim to your property, like a gold certificate for your gold coin, the Bea$t confiscates it under threat of force. The Bea$t has it both ways. This matches the prophesy, word for word. It has come to pass, via illusion, beguilement and trickery. Honorable competition has ended. In this physical world, all material wealth (and **You!**) belongs to **Them** (the International Bank$ters).

Chapter 24

Redemption and Remedy

"You shall use their laws against them." (Author unknown)

"Civilization is in a race between education and catastrophe." (H.G. Wells, author)

In reading this chapter, we again remind you that our use of the term "bea$t" is a metaphor only. This means the word is used as a common term replacement for something embodying vileness and greed.

Author RM once remarked on the most evil plot he could conceive. It was conquering and enslaving a nation without firing a shot. Why? If you physically invade, the people would know. They would be given choice: to rise up and defend or knowingly succumb. But our nation was defeated without a shot fired, with no one knowing. The chains were very gradually applied, with our looking the other way! With no violence the infrastructure was left perfectly intact for the robber barons to milk their newly acquired chattel. And not one of them (chattel) had a clue. Can you imagine anything in human history so ghastly?

There is no remedy by fleeing elsewhere. Virtually every other country in the world uses fraudulent liened bank notes. True, at the moment, some "third world" countries have far more personal liberty than do we. But, once America is totally subjugated, it will only be a matter of time before all people of all countries are welcomed into the Brave New World. You have repeatedly heard the term "New World Order". **_New_** World? **_Order_**? A New World Order where the Bea$t is sovereign? Indeed, you will be ordered! Either on the dinner menu of the Bea$t or simply commanded what to eat, wear, study, drugs to use, work, worship, etc.

Now that you know the truth, is there a remedy (defense)? Many who know the dots, but have not been able to connect them at first said it's hopeless. How, as property of the creditor, do you walk into the court of the creditor and demand justice? It's rather hard. On the other hand, you can use his laws against him as great philosophers have suggested.

Even in the law of the jungle (admiralty/commercial) as in the common law there is a provision for fraud. If material facts have been concealed from you, it is called fraudulent concealment. For example, if you "buy" a house and are told the roof was brand new, but it really was 30 years old and leaking, you would have recourse for fraud.

Additionally, there is the legal concept of unconscionable contract. Here is a definition and explanation from Farlex Free Dictionary:

> *"Unusually harsh and shocking to the conscience; that which is so grossly unfair that a court will proscribe it.*

When a court uses the word unconscionable to describe conduct, it means that the conduct does not conform to the dictates of conscience. In addition, when something is judged unconscionable, a court will refuse to allow the perpetrator of the conduct to benefit.

In contract law an unconscionable contract is one that is unjust or extremely one-sided in favor of the person who has the superior bargaining power. An unconscionable contract is one that no person who is mentally competent would enter into and that no fair and honest person would accept. Courts find that unconscionable contracts usually result from the exploitation of consumers who are often poorly educated, impoverished, and unable to find the best price available in the competitive marketplace....

Unconscionability is determined by examining the circumstances of the parties when the contract was made; these circumstances include, for example, the bargaining power, age, and mental capacity of the parties. The doctrine is applied only where it would be an affront to the integrity of the judicial system to enforce such contracts.

Unconscionable conduct is also found in acts of <u>Fraud</u> and deceit, where the deliberate <u>Misrepresentation</u> of fact deprives someone of a valuable possession. Whenever someone takes unconscionable *advantage of another person, the action may be treated as criminal fraud or the civil action of deceit.*

No standardized criteria exist for measuring whether an action is unconscionable. A court of law applies its conscience, or moral sense, to the facts before it and makes a subjective judgment." The U.S. Supreme Court's "shock the conscience test" in rochin v. california, 342 U.S. 165, 72 S. Ct. 205, 96 L. Ed. 183 (1952), demonstrates this approach. "......nullify any state law if its application "shocks the conscience," offends "a sense of justice" or runs counter to the "decencies of civilized conduct."

Was there deliberate misrepresentation? Were the people impoverished? Was there competition to the FRN with an alternative money system? Was there deceit? Was the entire population taken advantage of? Was it a criminal fraud? Was not the seizure and conversion of property (lawful gold coin) a criminal act? Would any reasonable man enter into the contract of invisible commercial liens? Would a reasonable man agree to give up half (50% taxes, including federal and state income tax, Social Security, and etc.) his labor (his life substance) for the privilege of mere use of someone else's property (FRNs)? Now that you know the terms, do you find this contract harsh and shocking to your conscience?

When the creditor ropes you in, even his courts would have to give credence to his own laws. But, we can't stop human nature. Yes, both the common law and commercial law provide defense against fraud, that's for sure. But there's always a judge who's totally sold out his integrity. While such judge might award you damages for the bad roof, he might deny you that defense of common right regarding fraud against the judge's boss, the creditor.

The real remedy is in the court of the People, with the People knowing the truth. For it is the truth that will set us free (as you will learn in a moment)! Shout the truth from your rooftops, in your homes and churches, in your neighborhood gatherings. It is urgent that you educate your family and neighbor. It is urgent that you take the truth everywhere you go.

Consider, if your clergyman discusses these truths in your house of worship, the house may lose its "tax-exempt" status. That's because it's dealing with the currency of the Bea$t. Your house of worship is in commerce! Hence, it made itself subject to the jurisdiction of the Bea$t. The law of commerce is NOT based upon unalienable rights. Your house of worship *__should__* lose its tax-exempt status. The Bea$t is in total control when you use its $limed FRNs. Heck, the congregation doesn't even own the building. It is liened by hypothecation to the Bea$t!

The only control government has on your house of worship is monetary. Any monetary control is the means to destroy (you AND your house of worship). By returning to gold, your house of worship would be **EXCLUDED** from government interference of **ANY** kind. It would fall into the common law of unalienable rights and out of commercial law of the Bea$t!

Now you know how and why the government places any restrictions on what you think is your unalienable right to speech. When connected with the use of the property of the Bea$t (FRNs) the speech and religion are in commerce and can be regulated.

You can't expect redemption in the courts of the bea$t. But even in the darkest night of hopelessness, there is always a ray of light. The courts of the bea$t have a huge Achilles heel that it can only protect through deceit. Its vulnerability is **_you_**, believe it or not. You see, the bea$t needs and uses you to condemn your neighbor. Even in the Admiralty court, it takes a jury (you) to convict a man. Even for a commercial crime! The judge will try to keep the truth of the laws from you. He will filter evidence reaching the jury in favor of the Creditor. That helps assure the defendant's condemnation. However, if you and others know the truth, you can educate the jury in deliberations outside the judge's reach. Jury decisions cannot be reversed. Consider that you are on a jury for a commercial crime where there was no injury. You now know he's been dragged in before you because of fraud. How can you now condemn him? It only takes one juror (you) to cause a mistrial or a hung jury. The cancerous admiralty courts are eating out the substance of men on the land. Imagine fellow educated citizens paralyzing those court$ of fraud! The bea$t would writhe. It will recede very quickly when the fear he instills in us all is lifted by truth and thrown back at him.

True, there are people in prison for crimes that violate the common law, such as theft, rape and murder. These people do need to account for their crimes. But what of the man imprisoned for only an action where there was no injury? What of the man who loses his liberty and property for growing hemp to clothe and feed his family? (The Constitution was written on hemp paper, now illegal.) What of the overwhelming majority of prisoners incarcerated at your expense (taxpayer) for victimless crimes? Hundreds of thousands are imprisoned for the same. Like possessing something (say medical marijuana) the creditor doesn't want him to have? Has such person violated the liberties and rights of anyone else? Should he be punished for an action without an injury? Our prisons are overflowing with the highest rate of incarceration per capita in the world (including China). In 1980, there were 200,000 in federal penitentiaries, NOW there are over 2-1/2 million. That's almost 1% of our total population! Most are imprisoned for"crimes" invented by the Bea$t, and **not** for crimes against their fellow man or as required within the common law. And we are a free people? And we intend to export that kind of "freedom" abroad?

In the meantime, do everything you can to acquire lawful money minted according to the Coinage Act of 1792. These include pre 1933 American gold dollars. Conduct your trade with them, whenever possible. We've shown that the courts have admitted and acquiesced that these coins are "invisible" to the government. Indeed, we have the documents of a man and his wife who sent in at least 5 such coins to California taxing authorities for payment of alleged and assessed taxes. Each time, they were returned with a letter stating that the coin was "an improper financial document" for payment (appendix H). Heck yes it was improper! It was actual money, not debt! If the government can't "see" these coins, how can it tax them? If you are operating within the common law with gold (lawful coin), the bea$t can't touch it!

We assure you that the greedy ones have beguiled you regarding investment gold bullion coins. They would have you believe that these current coins are equivalent or superior to the coins minted before the great 1933 theft. We promise you that they are not. Do a little homework. On the internet look up the Coinage Act of 1792. Study the Coinage Act of 1792 in appendix F. Discover the ownership of the metal of the gold and silver coins. Read how they were minted. Then go to the U.S. code Title 31. Read the specific sections authorizing coining of current bullion coins. These sections are 5111, 5112, and 5116.

Compare the fraud and illusion of the metal acquisition of current coins compared to the older coins. Your research will easily lift the deceit. You will see the invisible $lime infecting the bullion coins just like the currency. We have listed easy to obtain sources on the internet in the appendix.

Now you know that the Bea$t is heading our government. Its commercial law has co-opted the common law of the land. Our fathers, in 1933, were silent when our public servants allowed themselves to be severed from gold in favor of the Bea$t (FRNs). Their silence led us to the state in which we find ourselves. It is now the fourth generation that is paying for their sins. If you remain silent and do nothing, what about the next four generations? Will you have acquiesced to the replacement of common law with the Bea$t's commercial law?

Let's consider even greater violations directly to you and the whole of the American people comparing the effects of the laws of the Bea$t versus the Constitution. Many Americans have a religious belief. You now know that you have been compelled to bear the mark of the Bea$t by government. You now know that you have been compelled to cheat your fellow man by not paying him his due, and giving him a worthless and liened IOU instead. You now know that you have been compelled to steal from your neighbor that way. You now know that you have been compelled to participate in usury. You now know that your government has compelled your neighbor to do the same things to you. You now know that your government has stolen from you, and lied to you. You now know that all of this was done through Congressional legislative acts. You now know that your government has forced you and all your fellow citizens into crimes against your fellow man. You now know that your government has forced your house of worship into a tryst with the Bea$t, forcing it to use dishonest currency. You now know how your government limits speech within your house of worship through tax intimidation, and you know the source of government power to do so. You now know that $limed currency is based on usury, hidden liens, theft, and denies the ownership of property. Your very house of worship is liened to the creditor.

Please read the exact wording of the religious clause of the first Amendment:

"Congress shall make no law respecting an establishment of religion, or prohibiting the free exercise thereof"

So, we ask these fundamental questions:

> 1. *Would you consider the laws passed by Congress compelling these things to be laws respecting the establishment of religion?*
>
> 2. *Would you consider the laws passed by Congress compelling the above abuses to be laws prohibiting the free exercise thereof?*
>
> 3. *Is compelling your house of worship into usurious slimed currency an invasion of the separation of church and state?*
>
> 4. *Are the laws compelling your house of worship to use obligations of the United States and engage in international commerce an invasion of the separation of church and state?*
>
> 5. *If so, would these laws be a violation of the first Amendment restraint against government*

respecting the establishment of religion and its free exercise?

6. Have you and your house of worship been prohibited in exercising your religion and the laws of your God by these laws?

7. Has government granted mere privileges (tax exemptions) to your house of worship rather than your house of worship having unalienable rights?

8. Can you have freedom of religion if the $lime of the Bea$t is imposed upon you and your house of worship?

It is urgent that the American people awaken to the truth! The People are the ultimate court, not the judges of the slave master. Our elected officials are imposing $ on you. Are these officials now subject to the People's law or the rules of the Bea$t? Do you want to follow them like the Pied Piper directly to the Bea$t? We admit that many politicians, if not most, have been beguiled as have we all. Present them with the truth! Demand immediate return to righteousness with unliened money created from the labor of men. Demand the Treasury Department resume the coining of lawful money that was unlawfully suspended in 1933. The Coinage Act is still on the books to this day. The federal government has simply abandoned its compact with the states and switched the role of master and servant.

If the politician refuses, you must fully commit to the cause of the People. Work to **recall** all those who choose to continue sliming all people with the **Mark of the Bea$t**. You read above from the Congressional record, that members of Congress are the Trustees of the bankruptcy. A bankruptcy trustee represents and protects the interest of the creditor. It is his duty to be sure that all chattels are milked and squeezed on behalf of the creditor.

The People must reinstall statesmen into power, who will reinstall the treasury backed by gold and raise the People out of commercial bondage. When you have gold again in your hands, you will be the Sovereigns our ancestors fought the Revolutionary War for. You will repurify the blood corrupted by the ignorance of our fathers 80 years ago. You will not be chattel of the Bea$t, and you can once again truly live in freedom and free will.

Put the word "live" in the mirror. Remember, the mirror is the world of illusion. It's time we walk out of the illusion the bankers have created. We must reinstall our unalienable rights, and return these to the courts instead of the Bea$t at the head.

You have heard and read of the Battle of Armageddon. Is it a physical battle with nuclear bombs destroying people? Or could it possibly be the ongoing battle of planetary control by greedy men who invisibly marked you.

We humbly ask that you teach your family and friends they have been anointed with the mark. Challenge them here and now. Point to this little book for proof. We humbly ask that those who receive this book by electronic copy log on to www.NewPeopleOrder.com and remit $19.95. If you believe it is false, then we want nothing. The proceeds collected will be used for further books and education to assist us in the redemption of all of us from bondage. We will be continuing to post revisions and updated remedies on the site for purchasers. We also hope that the New People Order will self organize, perhaps through the website, into communities that will fiercely work to bring about the needed changes.

Please visit us at www.NewPeopleOrder.com and download a free e-copy of our sequel on remedy. We will continue to revise this as new information comes in, and you will automatically be sent electronic versions at no charge. We will be regularly posting your and our comments on the unfolding worldwide economic calamity.

NOTE: We have just learned of another means for population wide remedy. A new website has come on board called ***Complaints Magazine & News*** – www.Complaints-Magazine.com.

This site enables the one damaged by another the means to post the problem. The alleged perpetrator is also given the opportunity to respond. This site provides for millions of people to know what is going on, and communicate about it, outside the controlled press.

CM&N will enable millions of people the means to collectively pool not only personal, but governmental (agency and court) abuses visible to all. People will be able to communicate effectively to discuss redress. And then the burden in seeking redress can be shared by all injured and more effectively prosecuted.

EPILOGUE

As this book was being written, we are witnessing the greatest financial melt down in America, and the world, since the Great Depression. It could get even worse. There are warnings of a "calamitous" economic disaster. We have friends and family who worked all their lives. They made "investments" in order to retire and live out their days. Little did they know that what they accumulated was an illusion, make believe property. They were given the privilege of possessing it. But in truth, it remains owned and therefore manipulated by unseen hands. It was the property of the Bea$t. And the Bea$t is working the system beyond anyone's wildest dreams. Americans and people abroad are in panic now, fearful for their futures. Already trillions of dollars in security has been pledged out of the American taxpayers (you) to pay for the vile graft of others. The ability to provide for oneself in retirement is now questionable. The ability to even survive economically is now on everyone's mind. Trillions more in deficits are coming! The obligations of the USA now exceed the total GDP (Gross Domestic Product) of the entire world!

Where do the people stand? They are watching the government protect greed at their expense, and the permanent enslavement of our future generations. The bankers and thieves who allowed this fraudulent debit/credit scheme to grow into an all devouring cancer will be the only ones to make it. How? Their bailout will be on your shoulders.

How? In the form of higher taxes or rampant inflation robbing what you think that you have. Will the government come to **your** rescue? How could it when it is you paying for the rescue of the bankers and thieves?

Could this have occurred if credit and currency were backed by gold and/or silver? Could it have occurred if notes and certificates were truly backed by substance? Could it have occurred if our fathers 80 years ago did not allow themselves to be beguiled by the $lime of the Bea$t? Could trillions of "dollars" disappear if it was gold backed? Impossible! Now your accounts are backed by $limed paper only. And nothing backs that $lime but an illusion. Were the wealth both form and substance instead of make believe illusions, this disaster wouldn't be unfolding. There would be no hot air balloon or bubble to pop.

Greed is what accelerated the current unfolding catastrophe. Some are predicting that what is coming will be even worse than those grim Depression years. How could that happen? Billions if not trillions in "money" was created out of thin air, to steal wealth and labor from the entire population. This "hot air" was primarily loaned in the housing industry. The hot air rose. That "money" was distributed into all sectors of the economy. It was nothing more than debts, the workings of the Bea$t. The debts went bad. Hot air that rises doesn't stay hot. It cools off. That's a simple law of nature. It's now plummeting back to earth, worthless. All the monetary gains of the past years are based on fraud – and illusions. And, they're simply going "Poof", back to the illusions they were. That's what happens when you stick a needle into the hot air of a balloon.

At this very moment, we are barraged with dire warnings. We are told this is a crisis of "credit" and a shortage of "capital". But the "capital" in use is merely just more credit or lines of credit created out of the ethers. There hasn't been capital since 1933! It truly is a crisis of credit, because that's all that's out there, "credit" from the Federal Reserve Bank. However the "credit" is actually debt (obligations of the United States) owing the FRB from government and us. A giant tree grew without any roots secured in soil, and it is crashing down hard.

The whole financial system since 1933 is a fraudulent balloon, a creation of the Bea$t. Pundits are calling for honest "reform", admitting decades of mismanagement. But few are looking at the truth. We have been denied our unalienable rights and allowed our government to rob and steal for the benefit of the Bea$t, represented by the international bankers. The real mismanagement is "currency of theft" (liened FRNs). The real problem is not "**toxic**" mortgages as the government is leading you to believe. The fundamental problem is "**toxic**" currency, which underlies **all** of the problems. We could have never had "**toxic mortgages**" had we been lent substance (***honest money***) instead of the "***toxic currency***" (fraud/illusion), which is based on debt. Illusion, like a desert mirage, disappears. Gold/substance does not.

As the economic crisis unfolds, the FRB has admitted responding by running the printing presses night and day. You see, the government doesn't have to directly tax you to get what it needs. Simply printing more of the slimed commodity (FRNs) is their ticket. But what you don't realize is that doing so is really a clandestine tax upon you. Say you had $1,000 in the bank today. You leave it there for your future needs. The government simply runs the "money" presses doubling the amount of FRNs out there. Value is based on scarcity. With doubling of the FRNs you have just lost half of the value of your "money". What is the difference between Uncle Sam reaching into your account or pocket to lift half of it from you via a tax, or run the presses? The net effect of the toxic currency system is the same. You have been deliberately cheated. This could never happen with substance.

The only honest reform is to return to the Unalienable Rights of Man, where we exchange substance (gold or silver) for substance (labor). That would allow a truly free marketplace to weed out those who succeed and those who fail on their own merits. Now the system allows the Bea$t to decide who survives, for the interests of the Bea$t. Our fathers were silent in 1933 and stood by when their servants robbed them and gave them up as chattel. We are now paying for their inactions. If we don't act now, the damage will be meted out for yet more generations as the ancients warned. We cannot deny there will be much suffering until the change is made. After all, it took us about 80 years of false wealth to come to the catastrophe. It's like the movies where you sell your soul for wealth. You live high on the hog for so many years. But greed and power are in no rush. They know they will get what they own.

Our dilemma could take years to fix. But we must fix it. The alternative will be endless suffering and misery. Again, which path will you chose? Can you state that you are moving forward with honesty in your heart when you use the property of the FRB? Is it honorable to use the conveniences of the Bea$t, which use causes others to be enslaved? Will you have peace within yourself if you turn your back on your new found knowledge, and knowingly continue spreading the **Mark of the Bea$t?** Now, if we knowingly continue using and spreading the Mark of the Bea$t, except to survive, will we not be judged by our acts, not just our words? These issues can be resolved by demanding the alleged government to restore honest money, and succeeding! We must replace treachery and deceit with substance, with gold (and/or silver). We must have the scales of justice once again balanced by gold rather than the $ of the Bea$t. Witness now, in the world economies, the unfolding events that will surely affect you, your loved ones and communities, for the terrible price of using and being anointed with its mark.

___**In closing,**___ we would like to specifically spell out the nature of the Bea$t as we see it. It is the **interlocking** of the international bank$ters with our alleged "government." One could not do what has happened without the other. The bankers set up a horrific scheme. Yet they could not enforce it themselves. And the government could not have done it alone either. The interlocking "marriage" has created a monster (Bea$t) in which those who are sup-posed to be our servants have become agents for the hidden master (International Bankers). That's why until these revelations, the corruption could not be seen.

Bernard Madoff's 65 billion Ponzi scheme is mere child's play compared to the bank$ters. They have liened the whole (approx.) 65 trillion (2007 data) of US family assets (1,000 times what Madoff made off with). And, with only about 2 trillion in the M1 money supply (cash and demand deposits) to cover that amount of assets, the remaining 63 trillion is just hot air now contracting back to the ethers. Only those getting out of this Ponzi scheme early might have any "funny money" to show for it. (These figures are taken from the internet, including FRB money supply postings).

This is the greatest swindle, deception, theft, etc. in human history. It turned a nation's and world's) people into disposable chattel and enforced by their own officials. If you disagree with our conclusion, we humbly solicit your comments.

Finally, to our valiant men and women in uniform, please consider. *Once upon a time, soldiers were given gold or silver coin for risking their lives, limbs, eyesight, and future. Today, for your sacrifice, you are given someone else's (the Creditor's) property, which you have the mere privilege to use, and to pay taxes for the privilege of its use. We believe that you are worth far more for risking your substance (your body) and bravery.*

Sincerely and respectfully to all Readers,
Ronald MacDonald and **Robert Rowen**

Appendix A

July 4, 1776	March 1933
Creator ↓ Man (kings) ↓ State ↓ United States	International Bankers ↓ ↓ United States→ states ↓ ↓ man (chattel) man (chattel)

As is clearly evidenced above, when the Revolutionary War was won on July 4th, 1776, the Creator was above all, and the power flowed from the Creator to Man. Man then created the state and endowed it with power. The states then created the Federal Government and endowed it with power. Man, however, was in greater power/authority than his creations, the state, and the United States.

Today, the order of power/authority has reversed, with the Creator being excluded. As is seen above, the Bankers are in authority over the United States and the states. The created United States and states are in absolute authority over the people. And to our detriment, the people have neither authority over themselves or property, because people do not own anything, inclusive of themselves.

APPENDIX B

BIRTH REGISTRATION AND COMMERCIAL ATTACHMENTS WITH NAMES redacted for PRIVACY
NOTE: THE REGISTRATION IS WITH THE DEPARTMENT OF COMMERCE OR UNDER THE ADMIRALTY/MARITIME JURISDICTION/ AUTHORITY

See the word "Informant" on the section "***Children***" on page **79**. One who tells the authorities of a crime." Field 12A below.

Appendix C

The Master of Deception within the Courts

We wish to present you with an example of the master of illusion at his best. We do that with a further discussion on what has happened in the U.S. courts.

All judges, like the President, must swear an oath regarding the Constitution. The oath of judges who presided over the defunct Courts of the United States was the following (Judiciary Act of 1789):

"I, A. B., do solemnly swear or affirm, that I will administer justice without respect to persons, and do equal right to the poor and to the rich, and that I will faithfully and impartially discharge and perform all the duties incumbent on me as XXX, according to the best of my abilities and understanding, **_agreeably_** to the constitution, and laws of the United States. So help me God"

The current court oath (USDC) as well as the Appeals Court, and Supreme Court, affirms: "I, XXX XXX, do solemnly swear (or affirm) that I will administer justice without respect to persons, and do equal right to the poor and to the rich, and that I will faithfully and impartially discharge and perform all the duties incumbent upon me as XXX **_under_** the Constitution and laws of the United States. So help me God." 28 USC § 453

Notice just a single word change. We emphasized that change. What is the reason for the change? The original court officers swore an oath to be in "**agreement**" with the Constitution. That means agreeing to and adhering to each and every provision. That means plenary due process, lawful money, protections of each and every right not delegated to the federal government, etc. How could the courts be in agreement with the Constitution after the Congress stole gold and imposed a fiat liened currency? So, the oath had to be changed. The current courts act "under" the Constitution… "Under" what **part** of the Constitution?

We've already discussed the power to "regulate" commerce. That power comes from Article 1 section 8 clause 3. There is one other place in the Constitution delegating regulation authority. It is Article IV:

> *The Congress shall have Power to dispose of and make all needful **Rules and Regulations** respecting the Territory or other **Property** belonging to the United States; and nothing in this Constitution shall be so construed as to Prejudice any Claims of the United States, or of any particular State. (emphasis added).*

This is the only place in the Constitution mentioning "rules and regulations". There is no provision subjecting sovereign people within the states to the federal rules and regulations. These rules and regulations are only for territories and possessions. So we ask you to connect some dots. Are you subject to the federal rules and regulations? If you answered no, it's time to fly a kite. Now, if you won't grant that the power over you comes from commerce, search hard within the Constitution for an alternate source of power over you. Could the power to make "rules and regulate" over you be coming from this clause? If so, since you are not a territory, there is only one conclusion. You must be "**other Property**" belonging to the United States (or its creditor). Does not the United States have a need ("needful") to deal with and "protect" its property liened to the creditor? You have seen how you have become chattel (property). The United States has the power in this clause to make needful rules with respect to you (on behalf of the creditor). Does this clause close the loop for you?

Are there rules and regulations respecting FRNs and your use of them? Absolutely, and in every aspect of your life! This evidences them as being property "belonging" to the United States (by way of loan from the FRB). There are no rules and regulations regarding your use of unliened lawful coined money.

Note the words of art: "District Courts of the United States" (DCUS) and "United States District Courts" (USDC). They are two different courts. The DCUS started at the country's inception; the USDC took over at its bankruptcy. The latter is a mirror image. Is the illusion in the mirror really you? Has the oath been altered in the mirror?

The Constitution provided for three types of courts. In Article I, Congress had the power to create legislative "tribunals" (courts) inferior to the Supreme Court. Since you know that the power of Congress was commerce, these courts had to be commercial. Inferior courts included the district courts and appellate courts.

Article III created the judicial branch, the Supreme Court. It was vested with the power to hear Admiralty/Maritime, Equity, and Law (common law), as well as actions involving states and government ministers. Article III also empowered the Congress to allow its courts to hear real (common) Law (not just Admiralty/Maritime). The Judiciary Act of 1792 was passed under that power. It created the DCUS, which were limited to gold and silver coin as its money, as per the Constitution in its entirety. These courts were "in agreement" with the Constitution. These had Article III capacity. Courts created under Article I, the legislative commercial courts did not have full capacity. They were limited to commerce. The current USDC uses only commercial notes. Clearly, it is a commercial legislative tribunal. Created in commerce, that's all it can hear. If you go before that court, can you be anywhere else but in commerce?

Finally, Article IV gave Congress exclusive authority over its territories and possessions. Hence, Congress could set up territorial courts to enforce its rules and regulations regarding its property and exclusive zones.

Clearly, the USDC, appellate courts, and even the Supreme Court of today are acting **under** the Constitution. They are not acting in agreement with the Constitution, since they cannot "see" gold coin as coined under Article 1 section 8 clause 3. There are only two conclusions. One, they are acting "**under**" the commerce clause. Created under that clause, Congress has excluded them from other parts of the Constitution, including the gold clause. The gold clause was wiped out by HJR-192 in 1933. Or two, the courts are Article IV courts. These would be the territorial and possession courts. They would enforce rules and regulations "respecting" the "other Property" of the United States.

The only conclusion is that you are either in commerce, or you are the "other Property" of the United States or both! Who would ever notice this bait and switch if not searching for it? Is it not the epitome of deceit and beguiling?

This is the double proof (the coin and the oath) that the courts in front of us are different from our original courts. They (the courts) don't recognize the **Lawful** and gold money of the United States, or Law of the United States. They recognize only the opposite. So whose court is it? It is the court of the **Bea$t** (FRB). And since they are courts of the creditor, it should be patently clear what the Bea$t is. YOU are a debtor, owing to the agent (United States) of the Bea$t. You are chattel (property). You might not see the mark. But it is perfectly visible to the Bea$t, its creditor agents, and their enforcers (the courts).

This citation should sum up what has happened to the division of powers in America with the complicity of the courts and the commerce clause as 𝕿𝖍𝖊𝖞 **Own It All (Including You!)** reveals:

> *"The first sense of limited government refers to the ENUMERATION OF POWERS through which the*

Constitution outlines the jurisdictional concerns of the national government. This method of limitation has failed. The enumeration of powers is now a dead letter as a result of the nationalizing tendencies of American economic and social life, which the Supreme Court has accommodated through its interpretations of the Tenth Amendment, the Commerce Clause, the Necessary and Proper Clause, the General Welfare Clause, and the Civil War Amendments." <u>Encyclopedia of the American Constitution</u> – Sotirios A. Barber

Bibliography:

Barber, Sotirios A. 1984 <u>On What the Constitution Means.</u> Baltimore: Johns Hopkins University Press.
Berns, Walter 1982 Judicial Review and the Rights and Laws of Nature. Supreme Court Review 1982: 49-83.
Corwin, Edward S. 1928 The "Higher Law" Background of American Constitutional Law. Harvard Law Review 42:149-365.
Dworkin, Ronald 1981 The Forum of Principle. New York University Law Review 56:469-518
Purcell, Edward A., Jr. 1973 The Crisis of Democratic Theory Lexington: University Press of Kentucky.

The limitation of powers through enumeration "*<u>has failed</u>*".

On Social Security

FICA establishes a tax that is assessed by the federal government based on wages paid to workers. The funds collected from the FICA tax are used to fund the alleged "Social Security Trust Fund". Under a traditional employer-employee relationship, your employer withholds from your paycheck a percentage of your wages. The percent is based on the applicable FICA wage rate. These funds are then paid to the government. Hence, a tax paid by you, the employee. At the same time, your employer himself pays a FICA "excise tax" that is equal in amount to the percentage wage rate paid by the employee.

Social **Security**? The creditor had an ingenious scheme. He needed assistance in the dissemination of liened debt notes. It was important to hustle everyone into his plot. So, he promised to take good care of you if you made it to old age. He coined a beguiling name for the ruse – "social security". In exchange for your working years' labor, he would provide you with more of his liened debt notes later in life. He got the population to buy in to this now highly popular insurance scheme. It's popular because the government made it all but impossible to provide for oneself via the current tax scheme. Now, people rely on it (SS) just to eat and survive. The government pushes it in advertisements to the hilt.

But from another perspective, consider the following. All insurance is a wager. In the case of health insurance, you are betting that you might fall ill and need assistance. In the case of life insurance, it is a wager against death. Like all betting, the house has the odds in its favor. So consider the SS wager that you will live to retirement.

First off, daydream that the "product" (FRNs) you were given in return for the labor taken from you actually had value. It doesn't unless there's a beguiled soul willing to accept it. But worse, the government openly admits that Medicare and SS doesn't even have anywhere near the amount of FRNs that were forcibly taken from you.

Now daydream how you could have prepared for your retirement if you were left with honest money to do with what you wanted. Instead, you were given $lime, and there won't even be enough of that for you! For the younger generation, there is likely to be nothing at all. And know that there is no trust fund. The general fund, which is far beyond bankruptcy, has eaten it all like a cancer as reported by the Washington Post:

> *That's because, in some ways, the Social Security Trust Fund is a fiction. It technically holds government bonds, but – as a way of disguising the size of the federal deficit – the government doesn't count those bonds as debt.* (Source: http://www.washingtonpost.com/wp-srv/politics/special/security/security. htm February 25, 1999)

But even if there were something for you, how do you know that people will be willing to accept the $limed notes that your master (FRB) grants you? The house of cards may have fallen completely by then. The house has you by your most vitals. So, here's a question to ask yourself. Does government have the right to compel you into a betting scheme (even if there was substance backing the bet)? Does that not cause discomfort spiritually for the deeply religious?

Consider how you would feel if you bought flood insurance. The insurance company knew that there was a crack in a dam above you. Yet it dispersed all the reserves in bad loans to keep officials of the company in their cushy jobs. The dam breaks, your house is washed away, and there's nothing left for you, except what new premiums are coming in. Hardly sufficient. Would you not consider this criminal? Any difference with the SS Ponzi scheme? Is a Ponzi scheme not theft? Is this scheme not imposed on you? How does it vibrate with your spiritual views? And how does it feel to know that the one who is forcing you into insurance wagering is an agent of the FRB?

Appendix E

TO OUR BROTHERS AND SISTERS OVERSEAS:

This book is written from an American perspective. Please don't relax thinking that the malevolence you have read is restricted to America. At the beginning of Chapter 8 is a quote of one of the greatest men in U.S., if not world, history. Even in the 1700s, our American Founders recognized the dangers of the international bankers. With perhaps 2 exceptions, currency around the world is printed out of thin air. Then it's circulated at interest. You have to pay that interest, and there's just not enough to pay! The system requires someone **must** go down each year for the others to financially survive. Maritime laws of hypothecation attach to your possessions. Depending on your country, it could also attach to your person as well. Do you have a birth certificate? Do you know where the original is? Has it been transformed into a bank note with you as the security?

You are further affected because the treachery that is running the USA politically almost certainly interfaces with your country as well. Look at your fiat currency. Understand that your country is also a debtor, as are you. Follow the "money" or profit trail to understand the cause of most if not all wars (incited by politics), and who benefits.

The worldwide economy is an intertwined house of cards. More accurately, it is in a marionette. The bankers are pulling the strings in hiding from above. The world economy is crumbling as this book is written. The bankers can't lose no matter how the cards fall. Can you say that the international bankers are not running your countries as well, from behind closed doors?

The power to enact this law arises from the enumerated power to Congress (Article 1 Sec. 8 Clause 5):

"To coin Money, regulate the Value thereof, and of foreign Coin, and fix the Standard of Weights and Measures"

You might think that this gave power to Congress to "create" money. That's not what the grammar says. Let's use this phrase as an example: "Congress has the power to bottle Water, regulate the value thereof, and of foreign Water, and fix the Standard of Weights and Measures." The verb here is "to bottle". The noun is water. Water exists. Congress is given the power to bottle it (form or shape it). Then Congress fixes the weight of that particular shape (say an ounce, cup, quart, etc) to a set Standard that would be recognized throughout the country. And if foreign water came in, say in metric units, Congress could set an equivalent value on the weight of that unit of measure.

Applying that simple analogy to money we see the following. Congress was given the power to coin or to shape money. Money already existed. For millennia money was gold or silver. That's also within the common law. The shape didn't matter. What did was a means to adequately recognize the true content of precious metal in the alloy, bullion or nuggets. Rather than thousands of people taking precious metal to thousands of assayers, this power conveniently permitted the central government to be the universal assayer. So the power granted was for Congress to take "money" (gold or silver already out of the ground) and coin or shape it by fixed weights and measures. Please read the following excerpt from section 9 of the coinage act in that light. You will find that Congress followed its power exactly. It coined gold and silver (and copper). It weighed the coins. It affixed a dollar value to the standard of weight and measures. (And, within its power, it could assign a dollar value to foreign coin, based on precious metal content compared to American coins). After reading these sections, consider if the weight and measure of a paper denominated as $1.00 is any different than the weight and measure of a piece of paper denominated as $100.

Sec. 9. *And be it further enacted, That there shall be from time to time struck and coined at the said mint, coins of gold, silver, and copper, of the following denominations, values and descriptions, viz. Eagles–each to be of the value of ten dollars or units, and to contain two hundred and forty-seven grains and four eighths of a grain of pure, or two hundred and seventy grains of standard gold. Half Eagles–each to be of the value of five dollars, and to contain one hundred and twenty-three grains and six eighths of a grain of pure, or one hundred and thirty-five grains of standard gold. Quarter Eagles--each to be of the value of two dollars and a half dollar, and to contain sixty-one grains and seven eighths of a grain of pure, or sixty-seven grains and four eighths of a grain of standard gold. Dollars or Units–each to be of the value of a Spanish milled dollar as the same is now current, and to contain three hundred and seventy-one grains and four sixteenth parts of a grain of pure, or four hundred and sixteen grains of standard silver. Half Dollars…*

Sec. 14. And be it further enacted, That it shall be lawful for any person or persons to bring to the said mint gold and silver bullion, in order to their being coined; and that the bullion so brought shall be there assayed and coined as speedily as may be after the receipt thereof, and that free of expense of the person or persons by whom the same shall have been brought. And as soon as the said bullion shall have been coined, the person or persons by whom the same shall have been delivered, shall upon demand receive in lieu thereof coins of the same species of bullion which shall have been so delivered, weight for weight, of the pure gold or pure silver therein contained: Provided nevertheless, That it shall be at the mutual option of the party or parties bringing such bullion, and of the director of the said mint, to make an immediate exchange of coins for standard bullion, with a deduction of one half per cent. from the weight of the pure gold, or pure silver contained in the said bullion, as an indemnification to the mint for the time which will necessarily be required for coining the said bullion, and for the advance which have been so made in coins. And it shall be the duty of the Secretary of the Treasury to furnish the said mint from time to time whenever the state of the treasury will admit thereof, with such sums as may be necessary for effecting the said exchanges, to be replaced as speedily as may be out of the coins which shall have been made of the bullion for which the monies so furnished shall have been exchanged; and the said deduction of one half per cent. shall constitute a fund towards defraying the expenses of the said mint.

Sec. 16. *And be it further enacted, That all the gold and silver coins which shall have been struck at, and issued from the said mint,* **shall be a lawful tender in all payments whatsoever**, *those of full weight according to the respective values herein before declared, and those of less than full weight of values proportional to their respective weights.*

Sec. 20. *And be it further enacted, That the money of account of the United States shall be expressed in dollars or units, dimes or tenth, cents or hundredths, and miles or thousandths, a dime being the tenth part of a dollar, a cent the hundredth part of a dollar, a mile the thousandth part of a dollar, and that* **all accounts in the public offices and all proceedings in the courts of the United States shall be kept and had in conformity to this regulation.**

Appendix G

Judiciary Act of 1789 http://www.constitution.org/us-law/judiciary_1789.htm

Coinage Act of 1792 http://www.constitution.org/us-law/coinage1792.txt

Modern Money Mechanics, Federal Reserve Bank of Chicago http://famguardian.org/Subjects/MoneyBanking/Money/ModernMoneyMechanics/mmm2.htm

Federal Reserve Note definition Title 12, Section 411 http://www4.law.cornell.edu/uscode/uscode12/usc_sec_12_00000411----000-.html

Bullion and Numismatic Coins
http://www4.law.cornell.edu/uscode/uscode31/usc_sec_31_00005116----000-.html
http://www4.law.cornell.edu/uscode/uscode31/usc_sec_31_00005116----000-.html
http://www4.law.cornell.edu/uscode/uscode31/usc_sec_31_00005132----000-.html

Walker Todd working paper, Federal Reserve Bank of Cleveland http://www.clevelandfed.org/Research/Workpaper/1994/wp9405.pdf

Secrets of the Federal Reserve by Eustace Mullins
http://www.mindcontrolforums.com/fr5.htm

The Creature from Jekyll Island by G. Edward Griffin, available at Amazon

www.freedocumentaries.com

APPENDIX H – GOLD COIN TENDERED IN PAYMENT RETURNED BY CALIFORNIA TAXING AUTHORITY. (NOTE FIVE-DOLLAR GOLD COIN (INVALID PAYMENT) ATTACHED ON THE LOWER RIGHT OF THE PAGE)

STATE OF CALIFORNIA
FRANCHISE TAX BOARD
P O Box 2966
Rancho Cordova CA 95741-2966
Telephone (916) 845-7790
Website: www.ftb.ca.gov

Date:	January 19, 2007
Case:	
Case Unit:	
In reply refer to:	

Regarding: Invalid Payment
Account Number:
Taxpayer's Name:
Taxable Year(s):   2002 and all years

We received your letter regarding the tax year listed above. Please note the following:

You submitted an invalid payment to us for the 2002 tax year. The gold coin you submitted for payment is not a proper financial instrument and does not meet the payment criteria specified in Revenue and Taxation Code section 19005.

We are returning the enclosed document you submitted as payment for your 2002 tax year. Your tax liability, including penalties and interest, remains unpaid. To avoid further actions, please pay the amount due with a valid payment.

An accounting of the remaining balance of lawful debt owing is attached, as you have requested.

Please use the following mailing address:

FRANCHISE TAX BOARD
Accounts Receivable Management Division, Mail Stop A-455
PO Box 2966
Rancho Cordova CA 95741-2966

↑
$5 gold coin

Appendix I

Be Frightened, Be VERY Frightened

"I care not what puppet is placed on the throne of England to rule the Empire, ...The man that controls Britain's money supply controls the British Empire. And I control the money supply." (Baron Nathan Mayer Rothschild, of the Rothschild family international banking cartel)

It was an afterthought to add this section. We didn't want it in the body of the book to distract from the reality of the painful knowledge. But we feel it necessary to draw your attention to some events in American history. Coincidence? You be the judge.

1829-1837 Andrew Jackson, President. Strongly opposed to a central bank. He stated that it exposed the government to control by foreign interests, and would make the rich richer. Upon assuming the office, he called a delegation of bankers into the White House. He told them, "*You are a den of vipers and thieves! I intend to rout you out, and by the grace of the Eternal God, will rout you out!*" Jackson did accomplish his task. He dissolved the Second National Bank of America (back then banks were granted twenty year charters to print money). Soon afterwards, in 1835, there was an attempt on his life. The would be assassin's gun jammed. He pulled a second gun and it jammed as well.

1861-1865 Abraham Lincoln, President, had plunged this nation into war and heavy debt. To prevent bankers taking over a nation in debt, he issued debt free currency called greenbacks. He beat the bankers. During the war, the London Times brazenly reported that by that method, the U.S. would furnish its own money without cost, and added "That government must be destroyed, or it will destroy every monarchy on the globe." *Corporations have been enthroned and an era of corruption in high places will follow, and the money powers of the country will endeavor to prolong its reign by working upon the prejudices of the people until the wealth is aggregated in the hands of a few, and the Republic destroyed."* Assassinated spring 1865.

1881 James Garfield, President. *"Whoever controls the volume of money in any country is absolute master of all industry and commerce."* Shot by assailant shortly after taking office. He died of complications months later. Shortly before his assassination, declared that whoever controls the supply of currency would control the business and activities of the people.

1901 William McKinley, President. Advocate of gold standard. Assassinated.

1961-1963 John F. Kennedy, President. On June 4, 1963, he issued an executive order (#11110) to issue debt free currency backed by silver reserves held by the government.

http://www.john-f-kennedy.net/executiveorder11110.htm

It is widely reported that he made the following comment to a Columbia University class on Nov. 12, 1963: *"The high office of the President has been used to foment a plot to destroy the American's freedom and before I leave office, I must inform the citizen of this plight."* Assassinated 10 days later.

Coincidences or connected? We offer you the following quotes on the international bankers:

> *"Banking was conceived in iniquity and was born in sin. The Bankers own the earth. Take it away from them, but leave them the power to create deposits, and with the flick of the pen they will create enough deposits to buy it back again. However, take it away from them, and all the great fortunes like mine will disappear and they ought to disappear, for this would be a happier and better world to live in. But, if you wish to remain the slaves of Bankers and pay the cost of your own slavery, let them continue to create deposits."* Sir Josiah Stamp, British civil servant, economist, and banker. He was a director of the Bank of England.

> *"We shall have World Government, whether or not we like it. The only question is whether World Government will be achieved by conquest or consent."* James Paul Warburg (prominent early-mid 20th century banker)

> *"History records that the money changers have used every form of abuse, intrigue, deceit, and violent means possible to maintain their control over*

governments by controlling the money and its issuance." James Madison, 4th U.S. President

"The powers of financial capitalism had (a) far-reaching aim, nothing less than to create a world system of financial control in private hands able to dominate the political system of each country and the economy of the world as a whole. This system was to be controlled in a feudalist fashion by the central banks of the world acting in concert, by secret agreements arrived at in frequent meetings and conferences. The apex of the systems was to be the Bank for International Settlements in Basel, Switzerland, a private bank owned and controlled by the world's central banks which were themselves private corporations. Each central bank...sought to dominate its government by its ability to control Treasury loans, to manipulate foreign exchanges, to influence the level of economic activity in the country, and to influence cooperative politicians by subsequent economic rewards in the business world." Carroll Quigley, historian, polymath, and theorist of the evolution of civilizations. Author of Tragedy and Hope.

We suggest the following additional materials for your immediate education:

1. The Money Masters, video available free online
2. Money as Debt, video available free online
3. The Secret Rulers of the World, video available free online

4.http://www.clevelandfed.org/Research/Workpaper/ 1994/wp9405.pdf Federal Reserve Working Paper (authors' note, most revealing)
5. Secrets of the Federal Reserve by Eustace Mullins http://www.mindcontrolforums.com/fr5.htm
6. The Creature from Jekyll Island, by G. Edward Griffin, available at Amazon

After viewing these videos and/or reading the materials, you should have an even firmer understanding of world events from the perspective of those pulling the strings of the "puppet" governments for their purposes. It should also instill knowledge that those in power already control virtually all the world's wealth. But that's not enough. These agents of the Bea$t will stop at absolutely nothing to gain absolute and ruthless power over all humanity, from cradle to grave. No one is above being ruthlessly murdered. No nation is above not being used as a pawn to invade and destroy other nations in order to complete the plan. Disorder is fomented at will. Then the populace will beg for a New World Order of **ruler**$ to end the disarray that was deliberately fomented. Conquest will be achieved by consent, as per banker Warburg.

We, the authors, have concerns. But when one discovers truth, he must go with it regardless of the cost. Our Founding Fathers risked everything, including their lives, for their truth and to keep distance from the international bankers. The only protection for any one person is that the truth be known by all. That is the purpose of this book. Will the bankers make yet more martyrs with the internet able to inform the world at electronic speed?

"The Freedom From the Bea$t" movement must grow exponentially, and the consciousness of the population literally drugged by the $lime, will automatically rise. That consciousness, of truth and honesty (especially honest money), can and will shake off the darkness and **greed** of the bea$t. We certainly encourage a new order of people we otherwise call New People Order.

Appendix J

Administrative Horror Stories

To demonstrate the depravity of what the People face with agencies, we are soliciting horror stories from our friends and readers. Below are two true stories from RR's hair cutter. If you have a story to share, please forward to newpeopleorder@gmail.com. Please put in the subject line of the email: "Horror Story" so that we do not overlook it. We will be adding such stories to revised editions and future books with name omitted unless you make the request to include your name.

The following is an actual email that Ron Mac Donald received from Doctor Robert Rowen on October 8, 2008. It is not an unusual email but it depicts the problems people across this nation suffer through on a daily basis: Just to be clear, Robert has a hair-dresser, I have a barber. Just stated that for laughs but there is nothing funny about the events stated below.

Hi Ron,

I went to my hairdresser today. Besides discovering that I am even more gray, I learned a few things. Might be useful for the book, or redundant.

Where we discussed seatbelts, we could add;

RR's hairdresser was shocked when an administrative officer walked in and tagged her with a $2000 fine for her 16 year old unpaid daughter baby sitting the cash register for the family business. Her crime? No workman's compensation for her UNPAID daughter.

And in recent days, another hairdresser in Napa was fined $16,000. Her crime? On occasion she paid her sub contractors out of her own personal checkbook rather than the business's checkbook. Why did she do this? She had forgotten to bring in the right check book so she paid out of her own funds to insure timely paychecks. There was no fraud in her tax returns.

APPENDIX K

Do You Want To Get Involved and Help This Nation and the World?

Having read the book, we trust that you have a good grasp of the serious problem we are all in. The New People Order is looking for people who understand the problem and desire to provide assistance in bringing the needed change besides educating the public. Please send an email to IWantToHelpNewPeopleOrder@gmail.com, which is on the website, and provide your contact information including email and phone number.

Thank you!

Get involved, or choose not to get involved. If you are like us, we do not want to hear our children or grandchildren saying, "Look at the mess that our parents and grand-parents have left us!" No, let's be the generation to make the change. Let's bring the balance back to the Peoples of the World. If we do not take this upon our shoulders, then no future generations shall have the ability to do it, because the International Banking Cartel shall by then have ABSOLUTE CONTROL over all of humanity.